EVERYDAY FAITH

A STUDY IN THE BOOK OF RUTH

PHILIP DE COURCY

Everyday Faith: A Study in the Book of Ruth

Published by Know The Truth
P.O. Box 30250
Anaheim, CA 92809-0208
(888) 644-8811

Scripture quotations are from the ESV® Bible (The Holy Bible, English Standard Version®), copyright © 2001 by Crossway, a publishing ministry of Good News Publishers. Used by permission. All rights reserved.

ISBN 978-1-7360801-0-8

Cover art design by JetPath Media

Copyright © 2021 by Know The Truth
Layout design provided by Fluid Communications, Inc.
Italics in Scripture quotations reflect the author's added emphasis.
All rights reserved. No part of this book may be reproduced
or transmitted in any form or by any means, electronic or mechanical,
including photocopying and recording, or by any information storage
and retrieval system, without permission in writing from the publisher.
The only exception is brief quotations in printed reviews.

Published in the United States by Know The Truth, Anaheim, California.

EVERYDAY FAITH

A STUDY IN THE BOOK OF RUTH

To Lily,
my beautiful granddaughter.
May you grow up to be like Ruth —
a woman of faith and excellence.

CONTENTS

INTRODUCTION ix
1. THE ORIGINAL CINDERELLA 1
2. A COSTLY MOVE 13
3. THE ROAD BACK 25
4. NOTHING JUST HAPPENS 39
5. FINDING FAVOR 53
6. COLD FEET 69
7. CONSIDER IT DONE 83
8. EVERYBODY LOVES A HAPPY ENDING 97
CONCLUSION 111
ACKNOWLEDGMENTS 113
ENDNOTES 115

INTRODUCTION

There is an old *Peanuts* cartoon that shows Lucy, Linus and Charlie Brown lying on the grass looking up at the clouds. Lucy first asks Linus, "What do you think you see?" He goes on to give a very elaborate explanation. Then, Lucy asks Charlie Brown what he sees in the clouds. Charlie Brown replies, "Well, I was going to say I saw a ducky and a horsie, but I changed my mind."[1]

When we compare the value of our ideas and contributions with that of others, it can leave us feeling insecure. We can even start to sense our inadequacies when we read about the men and women in the Bible. Let's be honest: reading of the saints of old moving mountains and witnessing miracles can make us feel small and useless. In light of the exploits of our biblical heroes, we can wonder if our work for God amounts to much at all.

I love to play golf and I love to watch golf. I watch golf for the entertainment value, but I also like to pick up some tips on how I can improve my game. I find particular joy in watching professional golfer Rory McIlroy play. He is not only one of the best golfers in the world, but he comes from the same county of Northern Ireland as I do. When I watch McIlroy play golf, I realize that I have a long way to go! I can only hit the ball about half the distance that he does. Reading the Bible can have a similar effect on our souls. Seeing the great acts of the saints of God can make us feel weak in comparison.

This is why I am excited to bring you *Everyday Faith*. Our focus will be on the book of Ruth. In this short but powerful Old Testament book, we will find ordinary people who demonstrate faithfulness to God. Ruth contains no miracles or angelic appearances. There are no epiphanies or voices from heaven. The central characters in this story are not prophets, kings, or mighty warriors. Instead, the main characters are regular people like you and me. We will see how God uses ordinary people who express everyday faith, and that He can do marvelous things through them for His glory.

The book of Ruth has something for everyone. It is a human story about life and loss. It is a tragic story about bad decisions and bitter experiences. It is a heartwarming story of courtship and marriage. It is an encouraging story about enduring loyalty. It is a dramatic story with cliffhangers and suspense. Ultimately, it is a triumphant story which points to the much larger story of Jesus—the son of David, the king of Israel. It is a story for you and for me!

Come back with me in time to a dark and tragic day, when God's glorious provision was found to be sufficient for His people. We will meet three individuals—Naomi, Ruth and Boaz—who will demonstrate faithfulness in everyday relationships. We will learn about a God who shows Himself faithful to the widow, to the poor, to the destitute and to the discouraged. We will see that God can bless our *everyday faith* in ways that are greater than we can ask or think.

CHAPTER 1

THE ORIGINAL CINDERELLA

In my first attempt at a jigsaw puzzle, my mother taught me to start by joining all the edge pieces together to make the border. Once you have the big picture in place, you can fill in the pieces toward the center. This was good advice regarding puzzles; it is also good advice for studying the Bible. Seeing the big picture is essential in knowing how the details fit together.

As we begin our look into everyday faith, I want to provide a basic overview of the book of Ruth. I enjoy these introductions to books of the Bible because they help me understand the overall flow of the biblical story. When we study the Bible, it's easy to miss the forest for the trees. Learning some basic truths about the book of Ruth will help us to appreciate the flow of its narrative.

THE AUTHOR

We are not sure who wrote the book of Ruth. The book does not clearly state the author's identity. According to the Talmud and Jewish tradition, Ruth was written by the Old Testament prophet, Samuel. This is one possible and plausible explanation. Samuel was the prophet who anointed David as king. He would have been concerned about the Davidic lineage of the Messiah (Ruth 4:18–22). However, because the book does not identify who the author is, this is not an issue that Christians should be dogmatic about.

Ruth is identified as being a "Moabite" woman (Ruth 1:4). She was not an Israelite. She was outside of the covenant of the people of God. She had no claim to the promises made to God's people. According to the Mosaic Law in Deuteronomy 23:3, Ruth would have not been allowed to enter the assembly of the Lord. For a Moabite to take center stage in this story is an amazing demonstration of God's grace.

Ruth is described as a "virtuous woman" (Ruth 3:11). She exhibits all of the major characteristics of the virtuous wife described in Proverbs 31. Ruth is a spiritual model to us all, but she is a particular model to the women of the church. Sometimes we tend to focus on the male heroes of the Bible. We would do well to also highlight the many women in the Bible who were used by God in amazing ways.

Once I had the opportunity to preach on the subject of heaven. I spoke of the fellowship that will take place among the saints of God (Matthew 8:11). I talked about what a joy it will be to fraternize with men like Moses, Elijah, David, Jonah, Peter, Paul, and John. When I got home, I received a text message from my daughter, Angela, who is a diligent student of God's Word. She said, "Won't you want to talk to Sarah, Hannah, Rahab, Ruth, and Martha?" I texted right back: "Duly rebuked."

Ruth is a fascinating woman and we need to get to know her. Her story exalts the grace of God. From an Old Testament perspective, the book of Ruth anticipates the coming of Jesus by referencing the line of David (Ruth 4:18–22). This book encourages us, speaks into our lives, and exalts the grace of God.

THE AUDIENCE

While the events of this book take place in the days of the judges (Judges 21:15; Ruth 1:1), the book was most likely written several decades later near 1000 B.C. If Samuel was the author of this book, it would have been written around the time when David was anointed king by Samuel. The book of Ruth may have been used to defend David's claim to the throne of Israel. In light of Saul's jealousy and hostility toward David, it would have served to affirm David's ascension as king.

One of the key words of the book is the Hebrew word *hesed*. This word describes a love that is loyal and steadfast. We see the theme of *hesed* displayed in Ruth's steadfast love toward Naomi; we also see it exemplified in Boaz's loyal love toward Ruth. God's *hesed* is seen in His faithfulness to Israel through the dark generations of Israel's history. This book reminds us that the steadfast love of God endures to every generation and to our lives today (Psalms 100:5, 106:1, 107:1, 118:1).

THE ARRANGEMENT

The great Bible teacher Warren Wiersbe used to say, "I milk a lot of cows, but I make my own butter." I'm going to milk Warren Wiersbe's outline of the book of Ruth. He observed that the book unfolds like a four-act play. The words *weeping, working, waiting,* and *wedding* summarize four key events:[1]

1. *Weeping* (Chapter 1): This chapter is about tears and loss. Elimelech and Naomi move to Moab. Their two sons, Mahlon and Chilion, marry Moabite women. The two sons die and Elimelech dies as well. Naomi is left in tears, bitter toward God. Ruth is determined to return to Israel with Naomi.
2. *Working* (Chapter 2): This chapter is about Ruth taking care of Naomi. The two women are destitute and have lost their inheritance. Ruth takes the initiative to glean from the harvest. She works in a field owned by a man named Boaz. Ruth catches his eye and he shows kindness toward her.
3. *Waiting* (Chapter 3): This chapter is about Boaz, the "kinsman-redeemer." He is a close relative who is able to provide for the two widows. The women wait for Boaz to take care of matters so that he can redeem them.
4. *Wedding* (Chapter 4): This chapter is about the celebration of Boaz and Ruth's marriage. Boaz falls in love with Ruth, who is God's "Cinderella." He fulfills his duty and the two are married. God blesses Ruth and gives her a son named Obed. Obed becomes the grandfather of David.

THE APPLICATIONS

Like the rest of the Bible, this book is eminently profitable for "teaching, for reproof, for correction, and for training in righteousness" (2 Timothy 3:16–17). There are several theological themes here that apply to our lives today.

No person is outside of the reach of God's grace

The Moabites were enemies of Israel. The marriages of Naomi's sons to Ruth and Orpah should never have taken place. Yet the grace of God overcomes all that sin and disobedience. Ruth declares her love for Naomi's God and says, "Your people shall be my people, and your God my God" (Ruth 1:16). By the end of the story, this Moabite woman is embraced as part of the people of God. Not only that, but she is given an honored place in Jesus' genealogy as part of the line of David (Ruth 4:18–22; Matthew 1:5).

Ruth reminds us of the marvelous grace of God! She is God's "Cinderella"—a story of rags to riches. She goes from being an outsider to God's people to being in the line of David. Ruth's life is a reminder that God's grace can reach anyone.

Paul knew this truth well from his own personal experience. He wrote in 1 Timothy 1:12–16:

> I thank him who has given me strength, Christ Jesus our Lord, because he judged me faithful, appointing me to his service, though formerly I was a blasphemer, persecutor, and insolent opponent. But I received mercy because I had acted ignorantly in unbelief, and the grace of our Lord overflowed for me with the faith and love that are in Christ Jesus. The saying is trustworthy and deserving of full acceptance, that Christ Jesus came into the world to save sinners, of whom I am the foremost. But I received mercy for this reason, that in me, as the foremost, Jesus Christ might display his perfect patience as an example to those who were to believe in him for eternal life.

My friend David "Packie" Hamilton is another example of this truth. When Packie was an unbeliever, I spent time in his company and witnessed things that should not be mentioned. Packie was ultimately sent to maximum security prison for his involvement in crime and terrorism in Northern Ireland. His mother thought there was no hope for her son. But an older Christian lady encouraged Packie's mother that God could still do a work in his life and committed to pray daily for Packie's salvation. Fourteen months later, as he was sitting in his jail cell, Packie was suddenly impressed with his need to become a Christian. He opened a Gideon Bible and read of the gift of God's Son and the promise of eternal life. On bended knee, he gave his heart and life to Jesus Christ.

David "Packie" Hamilton became an evangelist in England, leading people to faith in Jesus Christ.[2] He is a living illustration of the truth that God can save anyone. His life testifies that there is no sin so dark, no record of wrongdoing so long, no crime so grievous that it is beyond the reach of God's grace. My friend, if you have not yet trusted in Jesus Christ, believe in Him today for your salvation. Come and experience the marvelous love of Christ for sinners!

We must live godly lives among the godless

Ruth lived during a dark and difficult time in Israel's history. It was a time of moral apathy, theological apostasy and political anarchy. There was no fear of God in the people's eyes. As the book of Ruth begins, Israel is experiencing a famine in the land due to the people's disobedience to God's covenant (Deuteronomy 28:23–24; Ruth 1:1).

Against the backdrop of this disobedience and darkness, Ruth emerges in a quiet corner in the kingdom of Israel. Surrounded by a society steeped in lawlessness, we find an individual displaying covenant love and faithfulness. Ruth's story is an oasis of hope in a spiritual desert! She proves to us that believers can live godly lives in an ungodly world.

Many Christians want to live in a country where God's Word is honored. Although there is nothing wrong with this desire, favorable conditions to the Christian faith are the exception, not the rule, in human history. Paul aptly warned Timothy that difficult times would come:

> For people will be lovers of self, lovers of money, proud, arrogant, abusive, disobedient to their parents, ungrateful, unholy, heartless, unappeasable, slanderous, without self-control, brutal, not loving good, treacherous, reckless, swollen with conceit, lovers of pleasure rather than lovers of God, having the appearance of godliness, but denying its power. (2 Timothy 3:2–5)

Jesus sent His disciples out "as sheep in the midst of wolves" (Matthew 10:16). He prayed for His disciples, saying: "I do not ask that you take them out of the world, but that you keep them from the evil one" (John 17:15). Paul challenged the Philippians to be blameless "in the midst of a crooked and twisted generation, among whom you shine as lights in the world" (Philippians 2:15). He reminded the Ephesians to make "the best use of the time, because the days are evil" (Ephesians 5:16).

In my childhood home in Northern Ireland, my parents had a picture on the wall of the little Baptist church that we attended. One of our neighbors (who was not even a Christian!) had painted it for us. In the picture, it was night and light was pouring out of the church windows. At the bottom of the picture were the words: "Shine through the gloom."

This, indeed, is why the church exists! We must live as light in the darkness, shining wherever God has us. Society today is throwing off its spiritual restraints, but instead of becoming despondent in this season, we must focus on being salt and light in our communities (Matthew 5:13–16). We need to tell ourselves: "I need to play my game—regardless of what the opposition is doing."

There is no coincidence, only providence

Ruth 1 tells us that the Lord brings the famine to an end (1:6). In the fourth chapter we learn that the Lord brings conception and pregnancy to Ruth (4:13). While God is clearly referenced at the beginning and the end of the story, the middle of the story has almost a secular feel to it. When Ruth enters the field where she meets Boaz, the text simply says "she happened to come to the part of the field belonging to Boaz" (Ruth 2:3). This is a pivotal meeting in the book, triggering a new course of events for Ruth and Boaz! Yet the event is recounted in a very understated way.

While the Lord is not specifically mentioned in this chapter, there is clearly a hidden hand at work. God's sovereign plan is unfolding in the ordinary moments of life. On one hand, this is the story of a daughter-in-law who goes out one day to get some food. On the other hand, this is the unfolding plan of a sovereign God who is accomplishing something extraordinary through His people.

During the first Gulf War, former Secretary of Defense Donald Rumsfeld famously said that the United States military faced three obstacles: the "known knowns," the "known unknowns," and the "unknown unknowns."[3] It is a scary thought that there are things that we simply don't know! Yet as believers, in every circumstance, "*we know* that for those who love God all things work together for good" (Romans 8:28). You can take that truth to the bank! There is no coincidence, only providence.

God blesses and uses everyday faith

When Ruth decides to return to Bethlehem with Naomi, she does an ordinary thing. This isn't a big story of the conquest of Canaan by Joshua or the walls falling down in Jericho. The sun doesn't stand still. It's just a daughter-in-law deciding to be loyal to her mother-in-law. But God uses it in great and marvelous ways.

Naomi simply prayed that God would bless Ruth's faithfulness. Boaz noticed Ruth's self-sacrifice and care for her mother-in-law. He prayed that Ruth's actions would be rewarded. He then became the means of repaying Ruth for her loyalty. Boaz was taken by Ruth's beauty inside and out. He blessed her and became her kinsman-redeemer.

Kindness and loyalty were just everyday actions, but God wove these actions into a bigger, unfolding story. He was working quietly in the darkness of those days through these faithful people. God uses people who lead quiet and peaceable lives (1 Timothy 2:2) and do what is right when it isn't easy to do what is right.

I'm tired of being bullied by those who proclaim that the normal Christian life is a series of miracles and healings. God can certainly do miracles, but they are not normal. Do you want to know what's normal? *Normal.* Raising your children, working hard at the factory, having a Bible study with believers, talking with a neighbor—this is normal. God's work shows up in oily overalls and kitchen aprons, in changing your baby's diaper and playing catch in the backyard with your kid. Life does not need to be a string of miracles.

You probably haven't heard of the late Fred Mitchell. He was the director of the China Inland Mission in the 1940s. A biographer wrote the following about Mitchell's life:

> He accomplished no great thing, his name was linked with many Christian organizations but he was the founder of none, he made no spectacular and inspiring sacrifices, he effected no reforms. This is the story of an ordinary man from a village home with working class parents, who spent the greater part of his life as a chemist in the provinces and who, on that ordinary humdrum track, walked with God.

On the surface, you may be unimpressed by Fred Mitchell's life. But he was marked by a love for an extraordinary God. In a similar way, there's nothing flashy or fancy about the book of Ruth. We find no angelic encounters, no burning bushes, no parted seas, no terrifying glimpses of the divine being. You might even say there is a hiddenness to God in this book. It seems to be filled with coincidences and chance meetings. But God is at work all along, behind the scenes, using faithfulness to fulfill His covenant.

Perhaps it's time to reconsider what we think to be spectacular. The everyday love of a mother, based on the cross, is extraordinary. The lifetime, faithful provision of a father is extraordinary. The birth of a child is extraordinary. The forgiveness of our enemies patterned after Christ is extraordinary. The willingness to sacrifice for God and country is extraordinary. The ordinary infused with grace is extraordinary. The expression of God's providence in every seemingly chance meeting and daily interaction is extraordinary.

When missionary Elisabeth Elliot lost her husband, Jim, on the mission field, she didn't know what to do. She started by cleaning the house and taking care of her little daughter. She recalls in her book, *Suffering Is Never for Nothing:*

> I really didn't have time to sit down and have a pity party and sink into a puddle of self-pity. I did the next thing. And there was always a next thing after that. And I have found many times in my life, such as again after the death of my second husband, just the very fact that although I was living in a very civilized house, I had dishes to wash. I had floors to clean. I had laundry to do. It was my salvation.[4]

Our lives will rarely be glamorous or spectacular. We will simply look like people who are doing "the next thing." But God uses that simple obedience for His glory. Dear friend, devote yourself to quiet faithfulness. You don't know where the story will end. You don't know how God will connect the dots. Just remain faithful day after day. Be encouraged by the story of the original Cinderella. God can take your faithfulness and use it to accomplish things you could never imagine.

QUESTIONS FOR PERSONAL REFLECTION AND APPLICATION

1. Do you ever get discouraged that God has called you to be an "ordinary" Christian? Do you ever find yourself longing for the spectacular experiences of people in Scripture? How does the book of Ruth encourage you in your ordinary, daily walk with Christ?

2. Who are the women of faith in your life who have been examples to you and have impacted your life for the sake of Christ? Name some specific lessons that you have learned from these women and take a moment to give God thanks for them.

3. Read Proverbs 31:10–31. What are some similarities between Ruth and the Proverbs 31 woman?

4. Is there anyone in your life whom you have considered to be beyond the reach of God's grace? Spend some time this week praying for their salvation.

5. Reflect on the providence of God in your own life. How have you seen God use the ordinary circumstances in your life for His glory?

CHAPTER 2

A COSTLY MOVE

RUTH 1:1–5

I once heard a story about a new bank president who met with his predecessor and said, "I would like to know what have been the keys to your success." The older gentleman looked at him and replied, "Young man, I can sum it up in two words: good decisions." To that the young man responded, "I thank you immensely for that advice, sir, but how does one come to know which are the good decisions?" "One word, young man," replied the sage, "experience." "That's all well and good," said the younger, "but how does one get experience?" "Two words," said the elder. "Bad decisions."[1]

I think this is true! Life is full of choices. Everything we do calls for a choice to be made. The Greek philosopher Aristotle has well observed: "We become what we are as persons by the decisions that we ourselves make." With every decision that we make, we become something more or less. The choices that we make end up making us.

Given that reality and responsibility, we must be careful about the decisions that we make. This is especially true when we are under great pressure in life. In times of difficulty and seasons of pain, we are likely to make rash and unwise decisions. Those decisions can have prolonged consequences in our lives and affect the people we love.

The book of Ruth opens with the story of a man who makes a poor decision in life. This man is Elimelech, and he and his family live in Bethlehem. In Ruth 1:1–5, Elimelech makes a hasty, emotional decision to flee a season of economic hardship in Israel. Seeking to escape the suffering, he ends up only doubling his family's sorrow.

Elimelech's poor decision ends up being a costly move. His family will endure 10 long and horrible years in Moab. At the end of these years there will be death and despair. Friend, I say this to myself and to you: *running from your challenges is rarely a good decision.* It is true that you may find a momentary escape from pressure, but it may lead you to greater sorrow and disappointment. As Winston Churchill said at the Battle of Dunkirk, "Wars are not won by evacuations."[2]

I want to balance the warning against making bad choices with an encouragement from the overall message of Ruth. God can redeem our bad decisions. While the book of Ruth begins on a sour note, it ends on the joyous note of a baby being born into the world (Ruth 4:13–17). What's more, the book ends with Boaz and Ruth's bloodline joining the line of David (Ruth 4:18–22). Ruth even ends up in the lineage of Jesus (Matthew 1:5). Even the messes in our lives can be swallowed up into the mystery of God's providence. By His grace and mercy, God can bring us to a better place in life!

THE DAYS

In the days when the judges ruled there was a famine in the land, and a man of Bethlehem in Judah went to sojourn in the country of Moab, he and his wife and his two sons. (Ruth 1:1)

The story of Ruth is set in the days when the judges ruled. This was a dismal chapter in Israel's history. It was a day when "everyone did what was right in his own eyes" (Judges 21:25). The people had thrown off the rule of God and were living in rebellion against His law. Moral apostasy and national shame marked this era. It was a most unlikely place to find a story of hope.

The "famine in the land" appears to be more than a natural famine. In Deuteronomy 28:15, God had warned, "If you will not obey the voice of the LORD your God ... then all these curses shall come upon you and overtake you." One of those curses was the prospect of national famine

(Deuteronomy 28:23–24, 38–42). The severity of this famine was seen in its duration; Bethlehem would experience hunger for 10 long years.

Pastor Alistair Begg observed that famines often serve as the background for God to do His mighty work:

> "There was a famine in the land," remember, and Abraham went down to Egypt to live there. "There was a famine in the land" and Isaac went to Abimelech, the king of the Philistines. It was on account of famine in the land that Jacob and his sons ended up in Egypt. In each case, the famine proved to be pivotal, a turning point in the lives of the people of God as it was in the life of the young man in the story Jesus told in Luke 15.[3]

Against this gloomy backdrop, the story of Ruth shines with hope. Witnessing the events in these four chapters is like seeing the first gleams of light after a long night. The cast of characters is a young woman named Ruth who marries an Israelite, a godly man named Boaz who fulfills his responsibilities, and a mother-in-law named Naomi who becomes a joyous grandmother. God will use these everyday saints to push against the darkness and dazzle us with His marvelous plan.

Given the bleakness of these days of the judges, we might expect the Lord to do something astonishing—to raise up a Samson with extraordinary strength or a Gideon with his army of 300 men. But the big message of Ruth is that, more often than not, God works in quiet places through faithful individuals. The real heroes are not always the charismatic leaders who rise and fall, but the godly plodders, the diligent domestic workers, the faithful families, and the quiet servants of God who live peaceable lives (1 Thessalonians 4:11–12). Tim Chester and Steve Timmins said it well: "Christianity is best served by ordinary people doing ordinary things with gospel intentionality."[4]

Do you want to change the world for Jesus Christ? You don't need a great resume. You don't have to conduct a miracle crusade. You don't need to be a political rabble-rouser. You don't need to do something spectacular. You just have to be faithful in your day-to-day. Pay your bills. Raise your family. Have integrity. Love your neighbor. Be faithful to your local church. Serve Jesus in the opportunities presented to you. It may not seem like much but within the sovereign plan of God it can amount to greatness.

You may remember the testimony of missionary martyr Jim Elliot. Jim was one of the five men who gave up their lives for Jesus Christ while bringing the gospel to the Waodani tribe in Ecuador. We know his story well through the writings of his wife, Elisabeth. Although Jim died in 1956, his life continues to be an inspiration to many.

But have you heard of Jim Elliot's brother, Bert? Michael Kelley gives this encouraging glimpse into Bert Elliot's life:

> Bert is Jim Elliot's older brother. He's the one who isn't famous. He was a student at Multnomah Bible College in 1949, and he and his young wife [Colleen] were invited by a missionary to come to Peru and join the work there. Other than an occasional furlough, there they have stayed. Now in their eighties, they are still there ... Over the years, Bert and Colleen have planted more than 170 churches. And when asked to reflect on his brother, Jim, Bert's response is stirring: "My brother Jim and I took different paths. He was a great meteor, streaking through the sky."[5]

Bert was not a meteor. Randy Alcorn describes Bert as "a faint star that rises night after night and faithfully crosses the same path in the sky, unnoticed on earth. Unlike his brother Jim, the shooting star."[6]

Have you met someone like that, who is always the same? That may seem boring. And in God's kingdom we do have meteors that streak across the sky—men like Luther, Calvin, Spurgeon, and Moody, men like Jim Elliot. We are thankful for them and their ministries. But do not forget about those distant stars—the unsung heroes in the church—people like Naomi, Ruth, and Boaz, who stay faithful in the midst of famine.

THE DECISION

The name of the man was Elimelech and the name of his wife Naomi, and the names of his two sons were Mahlon and Chilion. They were Ephrathites from Bethlehem in Judah. They went into the country of

Moab and remained there. But Elimelech, the husband of Naomi, died, and she was left with her two sons. (Ruth 1:2–3)

During the famine, Elimelech decides to move his family to the country of Moab, which is enemy territory. The Moabites had been a thorn in Israel's side for some time (Judges 3:12–30). Elimelech is driven by economic desperation. He may have had some good intentions, but the price tag for his decision would prove enormous.

This bold but bad decision had devastating consequences for Elimelech's family. Although he probably intended for it to be a short stay, his family sojourned in Moab for over a decade (Ruth 1:3–5, 20–21). By the end of their stay in Moab, Elimelech dies. His two sons die. His wife Naomi is left widowed and destitute, and his daughters-in-law are widowed as well. Elimelech went to Moab to preserve life, but instead he found death. It was a shortcut that led to a dead end.

Elimelech's choice was a bad one for these reasons:

1. *He ignored the negative example of Abraham* (Genesis 20:10–20). He should have learned from the consequences of Abraham's journey to Egypt. In an act of unbelief, Abraham lied about Sarah's true identity as his wife. That led to disaster—Abimelech took Sarah into his harem. Elimelech should have heeded the warning of this patriarchal story and avoided the dangers of acting in fear rather than faith.
2. *He read his circumstances wrongly and emotionally* (Ruth 1:1–2). He didn't view the situation through the lens of Scripture. He should have seen that the famine was a result of Israel breaking its covenant with God, and he should have responded differently. He was caught up in his circumstances and driven by emotion. He selfishly reacted to the pain of the moment.
3. *He did not respond in repentance* (Deuteronomy 30:1–3). He should have joined in national mourning for the sins of his people. God promised blessings if Israel would repent. Instead of dealing with his sins, he fled. Fixated on the circumstance, he took it into his own hands to get immediate physical relief.

4. *He lacked faith in God's promise* (Deuteronomy 30:1–3). It seems like Elimelech did not seek the Lord nor call on His name. There's no mention of him praying and fasting. Despite the fact that the name "Elimelech" means "God is king" in Hebrew, he did not submit to God's authority. Elimelech lacked piety and a godly focus.
5. *He abandoned the place of calling and blessing* (Ruth 1:1–2). Bethlehem was his ancestral home and belonged to him by covenant. He forsook it and went to the enemy territory of Moab. The Moabites were the descendants of an incestuous relationship between Lot and one of his daughters (Genesis 19:30–38). He should have stayed in the land of inheritance and promise.

This is an example of how not to make a decision! As a pastor, I counsel many believers who are running from their troubles. They often remind me of Elimelech who is fleeing to Moab. They are driven by circumstance and swallowed up by emotion. Running from pressure may provide temporary relief, but it is only momentary because the real issue remains. Like Elimelech, the problem is on the inside, not the outside. We need deal with our own lives before the Lord instead of merely reacting to life's troubles.

Dear friend, you may be going through some very difficult trials. You may be on the verge of making some bad decisions. Your circumstances may be complicated. But I plead with you: *whatever your Moab is, don't go there.* Don't make a hasty decision. Instead, meet God as king and submit your life to Him. Make a decision that is guided by Scripture. Seek His glory and His kingdom first in everything you do. Trust that He can bring you through the tough times to better times. Allow God's truth to have authority over your feelings. God is faithful to lead you, guide you, and spare you from making a costly decision.

Let's consider two applications from this passage.

Our individual choices massively impact other people

Elimelech made the bad decision, but his family ended up paying the price. We never decide to disobey God in isolation from others. You can't drill a hole in your end of the boat and think that it will not sink the people in the boat with you.

I want to admonish the men in the church. God has given you leadership in the home. Wives are called to express voluntary submission to their husbands and children are called to obey their parents (Ephesians 5:20–22, 6:1–3). Fathers must make good decisions because their families are along for the ride! John MacArthur once said, "There are some people in my life whom I refuse to disappoint." He was speaking of his wife, his children, and those who trained him in ministry. Who are the ones you will refuse to disappoint? Resolve to consider their welfare in all your decision-making.

Sin always takes you further than you want to go

Elimelech probably didn't intend for his two sons to marry Moabite women. He surely didn't intend for his family to stay in Moab for 10 years! Those who commit acts of disobedience rarely anticipate their far-reaching consequences. There is a process that we set in motion by our sin (James 1:13–15). When that process is finished, it "brings forth death" (verse 15).

C.H. Spurgeon observed:

> When Satan cannot get a great sin in he will let a little one in, like the thief who goes and finds shutters all coated with iron and bolted inside. At last he sees a little window in a chamber. He cannot get in, so he puts a little boy in, that he may go round and open the back door. So the devil has always his little sins to carry about with him to go and open back doors for him, and we let one in and say, "O, it is only a little one." Yes, but how that little one becomes the ruin of the entire man![7]

Let us learn from Elimelech's mistakes and deal with our own sins in genuine repentance before the Lord. Let us deal with the "little one" of sin before it grows into a man-eating monster. One of the laws of the harvest is that we reap what we sow (Galatians 6:7–8). The harvest of disobedience will often be worse than you expect.

THE DEATHS

> *But Elimelech, the husband of Naomi, died, and she was left with her two sons. These took Moabite wives; the name of the one was Orpah and the name of the other Ruth. They lived there about ten years, and both Mahlon and Chilion died, so that the woman was left without her two sons and her husband. (Ruth 1:3–5)*

This is a somber text. Suddenly and without warning, we are told that Elimelech dies. His two sons follow their father's unbelief and disobedience and marry Moabite wives. God's law forbade this type of intermarriage (Deuteronomy 7:3–4). No children are born over 10 years of marriage. The two barren weddings are followed by two funerals when the sons die, leaving two more widows and a destitute mother. Naomi is left without protection and without provision. She has no heir and the family line will die with her. It is truly a bitter experience (Ruth 1:20–21).

The stage is set for the rest of the story. And what a story it will be! Before we are done, we will see Naomi's loss redeemed through Boaz and her grandchild incorporated into the line of Jesus through David. Naomi will ultimately go from the borders of death and despair to the euphoria of seeing God's benediction upon her life in ways she could not have imagined. Naomi's grief in Chapter 1 is not the end of the story.

God's purposes cannot be thwarted by man's sin or disobedience. God never authors our sin, but He does govern it (Genesis 50:20). Sin has consequences but, because of God's sovereign grace, it need not write the last chapter of our lives. Even when we make a wrong turn, God is still in the driver's seat. God's wise providence is not held hostage by the foolishness of man!

Anne Graham Lotz tells this true story from the Scottish Highlands:

> A group of fishermen sat around a table in a small pub, telling their "fish stories." As one of the men flung out his arms to more vividly describe the fish that got away, he accidentally hit the tray of drinks that the young barmaid was bringing to the table. The tray and the drinks sailed through the air, crash-landing against the newly whitewashed wall. As the sound of smashed glass and splashing beer permeated the room, the pub became silent as all eyes turned to the ugly brown stain that was forming on the wall.
>
> Before anyone could recover from the startling interruption, a guest who had been sitting quietly by himself in the corner jumped up, pulled a piece of charcoal from his pocket and began to quickly sketch around the ugly brown stain. To the amazement of everyone present, right before their eyes the stain was transformed into a magnificent stag with antlers outstretched, racing across a highland meadow. Then the guest signed his impromptu work of art. His name was Sir Edwin Landseer, Great Britain's foremost wildlife artist.[8]

I love that story; it gives me goosebumps every time I read it. I love to retell it because it's a metaphor for the book of Ruth and for each of our stories. What we mean for evil, He sovereignly turns into good (Genesis 50:20).

Are you living with the brokenness of your bad decisions? I encourage you to go to Jesus Christ for forgiveness and mercy. Own your bad decisions and repent before the Lord. Ask Him to turn the page of your life. The consequences of bad decisions might not be removed, but God, by His grace, can write an exciting new chapter in your life that brings Him glory. God is able to turn your season of bitterness into joy.

QUESTIONS FOR PERSONAL
REFLECTION AND APPLICATION

1. The book of Ruth is set in the period of the judges: a dark and dismal chapter in Israel's history. Do you see any parallels from that time and the times that we live in today?

2. Our individual choices massively impact other people. Elimelech made a bad decision yet Naomi and his sons suffered the consequences of that decision. Who are the people in your life who would be greatly impacted if you made a foolish decision?

3. Elimelech reacted to his circumstances emotionally and did not read them through the lens of Scripture. God was not king over Elimelech's decision-making process. What decisions are facing you today? What Scriptures are you applying to these decisions?

4. The work of God is done by godly plodders, diligent domestic workers, and mothers and fathers leaving a legacy of faithful families. Read 1 Thessalonians 4:10–12. What acts of "ordinary and quiet faithfulness" can you engage in this week?

5. Ruth reminds us that even our messes can be swallowed up into the mystery of God's providence. God can write a new chapter in our lives. Are there any bad decisions that you have made in the past that led you to discouragement or regret? How does the book of Ruth give you hope for a brighter future?

CHAPTER 3

THE ROAD BACK

RUTH 1:6-22

Throughout the west of Ireland, the landscape is scarred by strange, crisscrossing roads that climb up into the hills and then suddenly stop. They have no apparent direction or destination. Further research tells us that these roads date back to the 1800s, when Irish peasants were cruelly forced to build them in exchange for food under the Poor Law. The majority of the roads, however, were roads that led to nowhere.

As we continue our story, we find Naomi standing on her own road to nowhere. She is at the end of a harrowing 10-year journey. Her husband's costly decision has led to a dead end. Naomi is left destitute and despairing, but God is working. As commentator A. Boyd Luter has well said, "God specializes in turning dead ends into doorways."[1]

Ruth 1:6 says that Naomi "arose with her daughters-in-law to return from the country of Moab." The word "return" is repeated 10 times in this chapter in some form (Ruth 1:6, 7, 8, 10, 11, 12, 15, 16, 22). Naomi understood that the way forward was to take the road back. She returns to the place where her family had first departed from God's will. As Naomi recognizes their mistake and runs home, she will experience God's grace in a marvelous way.

THE PATH

Then she arose with her daughters-in-law to return from the country of Moab, for she had heard in the fields of Moab that the LORD had visited

> *his people and given them food. So she set out from the place where she was with her two daughters-in-law, and they went on the way to return to the land of Judah. (Ruth 1:6–7)*

As a widow, Naomi lacked the protection and provision of a husband. She had spent 10 long years in Moab and seemingly had nothing to show for it. But Naomi had heard that the breadbasket of Bethlehem was full again. God had been gracious to His people.

The ending of the famine in Bethlehem was part of the cycles of sin and rebellion described in the book of Judges. The people would turn from God's ways and then face trouble. They would cry out to God and He would send a judge to deliver them. They would have a temporary season of peace and prosperity. Then their obedience would give way to disobedience once again. Within that cycle, this narrative finds God's people moving from famine back to prosperity. God had shown His faithful care once again (1:6).

In a way, Naomi's story parallels the themes found in the story of the prodigal son in Luke 15. After rebelling from his father, the prodigal son wasted his resources in "reckless living." He, too, encountered a "severe famine." He was pushed by dire circumstances, but he was also pulled by the remembrance of his father, who was a good, kind, and generous man. The son took the road back to his father's house and was embraced by goodness and mercy.

A Chinese proverb says: "The journey of a thousand miles begins with the first step."[2] Naomi's feelings must have been all over the place as she put one foot in front of the other. Prodigals often set down the road to recovery with some trepidation. Yet Naomi was both pushed by desperate circumstances and pulled by the faithful character of her God to take the road back.

It's not easy for a child to learn how to walk. It's even more difficult for an adult who, because of a physical injury, has to learn to walk again. My own wife June was injured due to a bad fall in front of our house. It took her a long time to walk again without a boot. For a while, she walked very gingerly and painfully. Yet those first steps were the beginning of a journey to recovery.

Dear friend, have you wandered away from God's path? *Let me encourage you to take that first, struggling step on the road back.* As Oswald Chambers says, "Leave the broken, irreversible past in God's hands, and step out into the invincible future with him."[3] May your desperate circumstances push you into the arms of God. May the thought of His faithfulness remind you that those arms are wide open. Jesus said, "All that the Father gives me will come to me, and whoever comes to me I will never cast out" (John 6:37). God is willing to embrace you in love and mercy!

THE PARTING

But Naomi said to her two daughters-in-law, "Go, return each of you to her mother's house. May the Lord deal kindly with you, as you have dealt with the dead and with me. The Lord grant that you may find rest, each of you in the house of her husband!" Then she kissed them, and they lifted up their voices and wept. (Ruth 1:8–9)

The phrase "she arose … to return" (1:6) uses the singular pronoun, signaling that Naomi intended to return to Judah alone. It was customary in that day for family and friends to accompany someone for part of a journey until they came to a break in the road. This is what appears to be happening here. Orpah and Ruth have accompanied Naomi for a distance, and it was now time for the daughters-in-law to go back home.

Naomi encourages her daughters-in-law to return to Moab, to their "mother's house" (1:8). That reference is unusual in light of the culture of the day. Naomi was stressing the strength of the mother-daughter relationship. She believed that the women's mothers would care for them in a way that Naomi herself could not. You can feel the affection and emotion in this passage.

Naomi then prays over her two daughters-in-law. What a powerful prayer! The expression "may the Lord deal kindly with you" uses the Hebrew term *hesed* to describe the loyal faithfulness of God. An Israelite was invoking God's covenant name and asking the God of Israel to bless two Moabites. Naomi wasn't sending the women away coldly. They had become to her like her own daughters.

> *And they said to her, "No, we will return with you to your people." But Naomi said, "Turn back, my daughters; why will you go with me? Have I yet sons in my womb that they may become your husbands? Turn back, my daughters; go your way, for I am too old to have a husband. If I should say I have hope, even if I should have a husband this night and should bear sons, would you therefore wait till they were grown? Would you therefore refrain from marrying? No, my daughters, for it is exceedingly bitter to me for your sake that the hand of the LORD has gone out against me." Then they lifted up their voices and wept again. And Orpah kissed her mother-in-law, but Ruth clung to her. And she said, "See, your sister-in-law has gone back to her people and to her gods; return after your sister-in-law." (Ruth 1:10–15)*

Naomi could see no other choice. She felt that her life was jinxed and she was now radioactive. The daughters-in-law would be better off cutting their losses and returning to their people. They were young and she was old. They had a chance at remarriage, and Naomi believed they should take it. At her age, it was unlikely that Naomi would remarry. Even if she did, her sons would be too young to take care of Ruth and Orpah.

This was a selfless act! Naomi would have been better off if the women stayed with her, keeping her company and providing greater strength and protection. In telling them to go back, Naomi was embracing the elements of her own living death. She would absorb the pain of their absence, but she desired a happy future for them.

Orpah saw the logic and returned home to her people. But in doing so, she was returning to the idolatry of her culture. The Moabites were steeped in paganism and polytheism (2 Kings 3:26–27). Orpah walked by sight, not by faith.

In contrast, the text says that Ruth "clung" to Naomi. The Hebrew term *dabaq* is translated "hold fast" in Genesis 2:24. It describes fidelity and oneness in marriage. Ruth makes a commitment to Naomi that is almost unparalleled in Scripture. She not only commits to follow her mother-in-law Naomi, she commits to following the God of Israel.

What explains such a commitment? I think the only answer is that Ruth saw something in Naomi that demonstrated the reality of faith.

Perhaps she saw a depth of worship or a character of service that drew her. She had obviously received Naomi's expression of selfless love in wishing the best for her daughters-in-law. Ruth saw in Naomi something that she wanted.

It reminds me of the story of Phebe Barlett, who was born in 1731. Even at the age of four, Phebe was deeply moved by the Spirit and became serious about her faith. Her parents noticed that she would pray five to six times a day. On one occasion, her mother heard her say, "Pray, blessed Lord, give me salvation! I pray, pardon all my sins!" From that day forward, there was a deep and lasting change in her life.

Fast forward 70 years to December 1804. Phebe traveled to the town of Westhampton with her husband to visit her son. She became quite ill. A man named Justin Edwards helped to nurse her. As he saw Phebe face adversity, Justin was converted. He recounted later that he "saw the dying woman calmly trusting her Savior." He said to himself, "Here is a religion that I have not, and that I must have." Justin Edwards went on to become a pastor and served for years at the South Church in Andover, Massachusetts. He later became president of Andover Theological Seminary. Phebe shined brightly as a testimony for Christ from her conversion at four years old until her death at the age of 73.[4]

God uses the testimony of faithful saints to draw others to Himself. Something of this dynamic must have been seen in the testimony of Naomi. Ruth must have looked at her mother-in-law's faith and thought, "Here is a religion that I must have." After witnessing Naomi's life of worship, Ruth did not want to return to her idols in Moab. Instead, she confesses: "Your people shall be my people, and your God my God" (1:16).

THE PLEDGE

> *But Ruth said, "Do not urge me to leave you or to return from following you. For where you go I will go, and where you lodge I will lodge. Your people shall be my people, and your God my God. Where you die I will die, and there will I be buried. May the LORD do so to me and more also if anything but death parts me from you." And when Naomi saw that she was determined to go with her, she said no more. (Ruth 1:16–18)*

This stunning statement of love and loyalty rivals some of the greatest confessions of faith in the Bible. We learn in Ruth 2:11 that Ruth has living parents that she left behind in Moab. She could have gone back to her mother's house. She could have been provided for in the land of her birth. Instead, she journeys to a foreign land and commits herself to an uncertain future.

Ruth is determined that, come what may, nothing will separate her from Naomi. Ruth wills to share in Naomi's future: her travel, her home, her culture, her faith, and even her burial ground. It is a staggering expression of faithful love, and it informs how we should relate to one another today.

Consider the cost of Ruth's loyalty to Naomi. Ruth is still adjusting to widowhood herself. She is still grieving. She joins with a penniless widow and heads to a land where she will have few legal rights. She gives up the prospect of marriage and future children. She commits herself to care for an older woman, even when she is in need of care herself. This indeed is an expression of love and kindness.

Note that it is God who is showing kindness to Naomi through Ruth. Paul Miller observes that "Ruth is God's answer to Naomi's lament. Within seconds of Naomi's charge that 'the hand of the LORD has gone out against me,' Ruth's hands are clinging to Naomi in a fierce grip of love."[5] That's a great statement! Perhaps the hand of God was not against Naomi as much as she thought. Ruth's love and friendship were evidence of God's love and a reminder that God had not forsaken her.

There is power in the companionship of a loyal friend. Proverbs 18:24 says, "there is a friend who sticks closer than a brother." Having a friend who commits to take the journey with us is a wonderful grace from God. There are Orpahs who don't take the journey with us, and there are Ruths who commit themselves to walk with us on the way. These true companions suffer our laments. They bear the cost of love. They love whether they feel like it or not. They love us out of the overflow of their love for God.

John Tucker elaborates:

> What the book of Ruth has the audacity to suggest is that a single act of heroic love on the part of an insignificant, ethnically alien widow was the key to the whole of Israel's future blessing. So per-

haps there is nothing more powerful that we can do for this sin-sick world of ours than to demonstrate, like Ruth, the nature of God's covenant love in our dealings with one another. Do you have any idea how many such lonely and vulnerable Naomis there are in the world today? We desperately need Ruths who are prepared to sacrifice their own desires and fulfillment to reach out to them in covenant love.[6]

It is a wonderful providence of God to look back on your life and see someone who has loved you like Ruth—a mother, a father, a faithful friend, or a counselor who has said hard things out of love. *Being* that faithful friend to others is an even greater blessing (Acts 20:35). We see such loyal love in the man who cares for an elderly relative, the couple who takes in orphans, the nurse who attends to the sick and hurting, and the woman who makes space and time to be there for friends.

Pastor Shane Idleman of Westside Christian Fellowship once told a story of such a woman. One night, she got out of bed and went downstairs when her young son came home and passed out. He was drugged and sky high. Her husband thought that his wife was going to go downstairs to kick the boy out of the house. Instead, he found her holding the boy—out cold—in her arms. She said that if he wouldn't let her love him when he was awake, she would love him when he was asleep.[7] This is a picture of real-life covenant love. May God grant us to express this type of faithfulness to others!

THE PAIN

So the two of them went on until they came to Bethlehem. And when they came to Bethlehem, the whole town was stirred because of them. And the women said, "Is this Naomi?" She said to them, "Do not call me Naomi; call me Mara, for the Almighty has dealt very bitterly with me. I went away full, and the LORD has brought me back empty. Why call me Naomi, when the LORD has testified against me and the Almighty has brought calamity upon me?" (Ruth 1:19–21)

With Ruth at her side, Naomi journeys to Bethlehem. Naomi's return, as you can imagine, is the talk of the town. The townsfolk are "stirred" (1:19). The author uses a Hebrew word which speaks of creating a commotion (cf. 1 Samuel 4:5). The gossip columns in Bethlehem had plenty to write about.

The women of the town ask the question: "Is this Naomi?" Their question may speak to the fact that they had not expected to see Naomi after 10 long years. It may also be a reaction to the harrowing experience written on her face. Barry Webb summarizes the scene: "Naomi and Ruth are like storm-battered ships limping into harbor."[8] Naomi may have looked exhausted, old, and haggard. The pain of her loss must have been plain for all to see.

In response to their question, Naomi says to call her "Mara" (1:20). This word simply means "bitter." Ironically, the name Naomi means "sweet, pleasant, delightful." Miss Sweetie Pie has become Miss Sourpuss. Naomi feels that her given name no longer reflects the reality of her life. She seems to have forgotten that God is able to take bitter waters and make them into something sweet (Exodus 15:23–24).

There is raw emotion here—no pretense, no plastic Sunday morning smile, no stiff upper lip. There is no papering over the cracks of her faith. Naomi is hurting. She is confused and empty on the inside. She feels that the Lord is more foe than friend.

The story is told of a minister who was making a wooden trellis to support a climbing vine. As he was pounding away, he noticed that a little boy was watching him. The youngster didn't say a word, so the preacher kept on working, thinking the lad would leave. But he didn't. Pleased by the boy's admiration, the pastor said, "Well, son, trying to pick up some pointers on gardening?" "No," replied the boy, "I'm just waiting to hear what a preacher says when he hits his thumb with a hammer."[9]

What comes out of our mouths when we are in pain reveals a lot about us. But there is a place to express our sorrows to the Lord. The Bible contains many characters who express their feelings with biblical bluntness. John Calvin explains: "we have permission given us to lay open before [God] our infirmities, which we would be ashamed to confess before men."[10] God is merciful to hear the prayers of those who are afflicted (Psalm 116:10).

John Newton, the former slave trader and author of "Amazing Grace," once received a note that said: "I am more disposed to cry 'misery' than 'Hallelujah.' Perhaps you feel that way, also." Newton replied as a wise pastor: "Why not both together? When the treble is praise and the heart humiliation is bass, the melody is pleasant, and the harmony is good." God can handle both our prayers of joy and of sorrow.

Naomi's language of being empty isn't the full story. Trouble tends to distort our perspective. With her nose pressed against the window of present circumstances, all Naomi could see was that the hand of God had gone out against her. She only saw her affliction without advancement. She was missing the big picture of what God was doing.

Naomi's trials had already borne some good fruits. The adversity she had experienced had driven her back to God. Her desperate circumstances had produced a wonderful friendship with Ruth. Her dire situation left her in need of a kinsman-redeemer, which would lead to Boaz marrying Ruth. This was only the beginning of God's gracious work in her life. Note where the story ends: Boaz marries Ruth. They have a son, and that son becomes the grandfather of King David (Ruth 4:17–22). God makes a covenant with David that through him a kingdom will be established forever (2 Samuel 7:15–16). Dale Ralph Davis has well said, "none of us know enough to say that God doesn't know what He is doing."[11] Through the story of Naomi's painful affliction, God was working to establish His kingdom!

In 1662, England's Great Ejection resulted in conservative, Bible-believing pastors being banished from their churches. Overnight, these men lost their pulpits and their incomes. Their faithfulness to preach the gospel cost them their ministries and their ability to feed their families. The law forbade them to come within five miles of their churches. It was a time of intense persecution.

One of those banished pastors was Thomas Watson. Watson had lost his position and all of his possessions. While enduring these things, he wrote a small book to encourage his fellow dispossessed pastors. This book was entitled *All Things for Good,* which is of course based on Romans 8:28: "And we know that for those who love God all things work together for good, for those who are called according to his purpose."

The first chapter of this book is entitled, "The Best Things Work for the Godly." The second chapter is entitled, "The Worst Things Work for the Godly." Watson gives the following perspective on adversity:

> As ploughing prepares the earth for a crop, so afflictions prepare and make us meet for glory. The painter lays his gold upon dark colors—so God first lays the dark colors of affliction, and then He lays the golden color of glory ... Thus we see afflictions are not harmful—but beneficial, to the saints. We should not so much look at the evil of affliction, as the good; not so much at the dark side of the cloud, as the light. The worst that God does to His children, is to whip them to heaven![12]

Naomi would eventually come to learn this perspective. The worst things in life work for good to the godly. Think of an open face watch, where you can see the intricate workings of the inner mechanism. The wheels move contrary to each other, but they all work in unison to carry out the movements of the watch. There are things in life that seem to be contrary to the godly. But these are part of the wonderful providence of God that will bring blessing to the godly in the end.

THE PROVIDENCE

> *So Naomi returned, and Ruth the Moabite her daughter-in-law with her, who returned from the country of Moab. And they came to Bethlehem at the beginning of barley harvest. (Ruth 1:22)*

The author goes back in time in order to move the story forward. He rewinds the movie to make an important point. It was harvest time in Bethlehem, and the barley harvest would require a large number of workers and reapers. The destitute could find fields to glean in (Leviticus 19:9–10, 23:22). Ruth will find work in the fields and meet Boaz. Better days are coming. The text is already moving us from the theme of bitter circumstances to the hope of sweet redemption.

God's timing is perfect! John Flavel wrote that "we find a multitude of providences so timed to a minute, that had they occurred just a little sooner or a little later, they had signified but little."[13] Think of the biblical stories that displayed God's perfect timing:

- When Saul was looking for lost donkeys, he met Samuel at the appointed time set by God (1 Samuel 9:3, 15–17, 24).
- The arrow shot by a soldier at random had the exact direction and timing necessary to strike wicked King Ahab in a tiny joint in his armor, fulfilling a prophecy (2 Chronicles 18:16, 33).
- As soon as Peter denied Jesus for the third time, the rooster in the courtyard crowed twice, fulfilling Jesus' prophecy (Matthew 26:74–75).
- The ram was caught in the thicket precisely when Abraham was about to offer up Isaac (Genesis 22:10–13).[14]

Centuries later, the town of Bethlehem was met with another well-timed arrival. Galatians 4:6–7 says: "But when the fullness of time had come, God sent forth his Son, born of woman, born under the law, to redeem those who were under the law, so that we might receive adoption as sons." God prepared the whole world for the coming of His Son, Jesus Christ. God is never late in fulfilling His promises!

Dear friend, waiting on the Lord can be a challenge. Yet God shows His faithfulness to those who trust in Him. A friend of the great preacher Philip Brooks called on him and found him impatiently pacing the floor. His friend asked what the trouble was. Dr. Brooks exclaimed, "The trouble is that I am in a hurry, and God is not!"[15] Let us learn to wait on the perfect timing of God.

Perhaps it's been a long time since you walked closely with the Lord. Maybe you've been spiritually dry for some time and uninterested in pursuing the things of God. You may even be dealing with the consequences of sin in a way that has made life bitter. I want to encourage you that you can always take the road back. Like Naomi, you can return to your God and find that where sin abounds, grace abounds all the more (Romans 5:20).

In 2010, Sandra Bullock won the Academy Award for Best Actress for her portrayal of Leigh Ann Tuohy in the movie, *The Blind Side*.

The film chronicles a Christian family who took in a young man and gave him the chance to reach his God-given potential. Michael Oher went on to become the first-round NFL draft pick for the Baltimore Ravens in 2009. At a fundraiser, Sean Tuohy shared how the transformation of his family and Michael all started with two words. When they spotted Michael walking along the road on a cold November morning in shorts and a T-shirt, Leigh Ann Tuohy uttered the words: "Turn around." They turned the car around, put Michael in the car, and ultimately adopted him into their family. Those same two words can change anyone's life. Your change of direction can begin an exciting new journey.[16]

Whatever your situation may be today, a great story of change can be two words away. *Turn around.* Take the road back to God's blessing. Admit your folly. Confess your sin. Take the first step back and that will lead to other steps. Through the gospel of Jesus Christ, God can take your adversity and produce something good. God can take the bitterness of your life and turn it into something sweet.

QUESTIONS FOR PERSONAL APPLICATION AND REFLECTION

1. Many of us have loved ones who are spiritual prodigals. They have made bad decisions and strayed from the ways of the Lord. The book of Ruth teaches us that what seems like the end can be turned, in God's providence, into a brand-new beginning. Is there someone in your life whom you pray will return to the ways of the Lord? How will you pray and prepare for his or her return?

2. Ruth is an example of *hesed*, covenant love. How can you demonstrate this covenant faithfulness in your relationships today? Is there a particular relationship that the Lord is leading you to demonstrate *hesed* in?

3. Ruth changed the world by demonstrating faithfulness to her mother-in-law. What ordinary acts of faithfulness is God calling you to fulfill this week?

4. Who are the people in your life who have been faithful companions on your spiritual journey? How can you be this type of faithful friend to someone else?

5. Take a moment to pray for someone in your church who is going through difficulties. Ask the Lord to strengthen their faith. Consider writing them a kind note or word of encouragement this week and letting them know that you are praying for them.

CHAPTER 4

NOTHING JUST HAPPENS

RUTH 2:1-3

Looking back on his path in life and his several brushes with death, Winston Churchill said: "One can see how lucky I was. Over me beat invisible wings." His near fatal experiences involved plane crashes, hand-to-hand combat in wartime, and being run over by a car in New York.

The best example of his good fortune occurred during the Boer War in South Africa. Churchill was there as a war correspondent for *The Morning Post*. While traveling to the war front on a troop train, he was captured by the Boers and taken to a prison in Pretoria.

After three weeks in prison, Churchill escaped. Being on the run for some time, he was tired, hungry and lost. He threw caution to the wind and knocked on the door of a random house saying he was a Dutch clergyman. Amazingly, the house he picked was the only dwelling in a 20-mile radius that belonged to an Englishman—a man who opposed the Boers. His fellow countryman hid Churchill in a mine shaft until an escape route could be plotted.

It would seem that Winston Churchill had his fair share of good fortune. A friend of the family would later say: "Again and again, watching his life and fortune, it has seemed to me Winston had a private wire with fate."[1] But was it sheer luck or cold fate that protected Winston Churchill for his destiny as Britain's savior during World War II? Did mere coincidence and happenstance author this man's striking story?

I think not. We who have come to appreciate the critical role Winston Churchill played in world history have no trouble believing that God was at work preserving the life of this man so that he might confront the evil of Nazism. The invisible wings that beat over Churchill were undoubtedly what the Christian calls "the providence of God."

Providence is the belief that God controls every aspect of His creation. It is the conviction that God works in human history to accomplish His perfect, holy will (Matthew 6:10). J. Vernon McGee has well stated: "Providence is the hand of God in the glove of human events."[2] God is sovereign over every moment and every molecule. He uses every movement in creation to fulfill His good purpose.

The doctrine of God's providence is taught in passages such as:

- Psalm 115:3 – "Our God is in the heavens; he does all that he pleases."
- Proverbs 16:33 – "The lot is cast into the lap, but its every decision is from the Lord."
- Proverbs 21:1 – "The king's heart is a stream of water in the hand of the Lord; he turns it wherever he will."
- Ephesians 1:11 – "In him we have obtained an inheritance, having been predestined according to the purpose of him who works all things according to the counsel of his will …"

From a Christian worldview, there is no such thing as luck, fate or chance. John Calvin said that "fortune and chance are heathen terms."[3] According to the Bible, life has purpose. History has direction. Choice has meaning. Questions have answers. Every day is a link in a chain of events that is assembled by a wise and sovereign God. Life is not, as Bertrand Russell said, "the outcome of accidental collocations of atoms."[4] God is on His throne and He is ruling over all!

The doctrine of God's providence is on full display in the story of Ruth. Tongue-in-cheek, the writer of this book tells us that Ruth "happened to come to the part of the field belonging to Boaz" (Ruth 2:3). This was the man who would eventually redeem Ruth and Naomi from poverty through levirate marriage (Ruth 3:9–11, 4:13–14).

What a coincidence? No, what a providence! Nothing just happens in life. God is up to something in the most mundane of circumstances.

While the first chapter of Ruth was dominated by three women, the focus now shifts in Chapter 2. Here we have the introduction of the man Boaz, who was of the clan of Elimelech. The narrative will move from a focus on the relationship between Ruth and Naomi to a focus on the relationship between Ruth and Boaz. The story will lead to a marriage and a child and a descendant of David. It all starts with a seemingly chance meeting.

THE IN-LAW

Now Naomi had a relative of her husband's, a worthy man of the clan of Elimelech, whose name was Boaz. (Ruth 2:1)

Here we are introduced to Boaz, a relative of Naomi. His name literally means "in him is strength." Boaz is further described in the text as a "worthy man" (1:1). This can be translated "a man of valor" (Judges 6:12, 11:1). What a great description of a godly man! John Currid writes, "The Hebrew word used here is not the usual one for 'man', but rather it is a term meaning a 'mighty one'; the author employs the word to underscore Boaz's manliness."[5] Boaz was a manly man, inside and out.

A needle is being threaded here by the author. The reader is introduced to Boaz (2:1) before Boaz is introduced to Ruth (2:3). We are given this information so that we may correctly grasp the significance of Boaz and Ruth's meeting in the field. We are to understand this seemingly chance event as nothing less than God's providential care for Ruth and Naomi.

In Chapter 1, Naomi urged Ruth to go back to Moab (Ruth 1:8–14). Ruth refused to listen and committed herself to Naomi as an expression of *hesed* love. In Chapter 2, we will come to see God's *hesed* love for Ruth the Moabite. Ruth will experience God's kindness through the provision of Boaz.

God had lined up for Ruth a man marked by spiritual stature. David Atkinson describes him as "a man of integrity, a man of influence, a man of means."[6] Boaz had a backbone, not a wishbone! He was a strong follower of the God of Israel. He obeyed God's law even during the days of the judges. Boaz was Ruth's knight in shining armor.

Remember that Ruth had already embraced the idea that her days of marriage were over. She had thrown in her lot with the widow Naomi. I'm sure that she had pretty much given up on the idea that she would ever meet a Boaz. And yet God is able to do "exceedingly abundantly above all that we ask or think" (Ephesians 3:20).

I want to bring this word of encouragement to young, single women in the church. You may be longing for marriage but you feel that the dream may be passing. Perhaps you think that it's not going to happen. In the meantime, you are keeping yourself pure and walking in faithfulness with God. I'm not making you a guarantee where there is none in the Bible. But I do want to encourage you not to give up! Ruth continued to be loyal and faithful to her mother-in-law, and that is one of the qualities that attracted Boaz to Ruth. Don't become discouraged and don't doubt the goodness of God. Pray, work, and be your best self. Trust yourself to the providence of God. You may be surprised as to what is just around the corner.

And guys, can I exhort you? Don't be a bozo; be a Boaz! This is the kind of man that you want to be. This is a man of spiritual strength, and you should aspire to follow his example. Pursue integrity, dependability, and trustworthy character. Be a man of spiritual substance and strength. Don't follow the trends of an ungodly society. Learn to grow in true godliness and spiritual maturity. Devote yourself to walking with the Lord. God may bring into your life a seemingly chance meeting that changes the course of your life. You may find yourself in the middle of a wonderful story!

Rowland Bingham, founder of the Sudan Interior Mission, was once seriously injured in an car accident and rushed to a hospital. The next day, when he regained consciousness, he asked the nurse what he was doing there. "Don't try to talk now; just rest," she replied, explaining, "you have been in an accident." Dr. Bingham exclaimed, "Accident? Accident! There are no accidents in the life of a Christian. This is just an incident in God's perfect leading."[7]

The meeting between Ruth and Boaz may have looked like an accident, a random meeting in the field. But God in His providence had perfectly arranged the details of this moment. Be careful how you read your present circumstances. God's gracious blessing may be just around the corner!

THE INITIATIVE

And Ruth the Moabite said to Naomi, "Let me go to the field and glean among the ears of grain after him in whose sight I shall find favor." And she said to her, "Go, my daughter." (Ruth 2:2)

This is a bold move! Ruth is a plucky lady, a gutsy gal. She is a woman who doesn't take life lying down. After all the tears and funerals of Chapter 1, she sets out to make the best of a bad situation. Although she is in Naomi's hometown, she doesn't wait for Naomi to serve her. Instead, Ruth takes the initiative to serve Naomi.

Ruth doesn't wait. She doesn't gripe or cast blame. Instead, she acts immediately upon arriving in Bethlehem, creating a plan of action to care for herself and Naomi. She sets out to see if God in His kind providence would bring a new day.

Leviticus 19:9–10 says:

> When you reap the harvest of your land, you shall not reap your field right up to its edge, neither shall you gather the gleanings after your harvest. And you shall not strip your vineyard bare, neither shall you gather the fallen grapes of your vineyard. You shall leave them for the poor and for the sojourner: I am the LORD your God.

Deuteronomy 24:19–21 also says:

> When you reap your harvest in your field and forget a sheaf in the field, you shall not go back to get it. It shall be for the sojourner, the fatherless, and the widow, that the LORD your God may bless you in all the work of your hands. When you beat your olive trees, you shall not go over them again. It shall be for the sojourner, the

fatherless, and the widow. When you gather the grapes of your vineyard, you shall not strip it afterward. It shall be for the sojourner, the fatherless, and the widow.

It seems like Ruth had heard of these provisions for the poor in God's law. Perhaps Ruth had seen others going to glean in the field. She senses this may be a solution for her and Naomi. Ruth gets to work seeking to make ends meet. She is not looking for a handout but a hand up. Ruth is smart, forward, selfless, hardworking, trusting, and hopeful. Ruth is a go-getter. I love her initiative!

This challenges me. Friend, I want you to be challenged by this as well. If you find yourself in the midst of tough circumstances, let me encourage you to take the initiative. Young men, I want to share this thought especially for you. Life does not land in your lap. Have a plan of action. Work hard, be humble, be smart, be tenacious. Start low, shoot high, and trust God with the results!

I'm tired of hearing a view of the sovereignty of God that sounds more like fatalism than a biblical understanding of providence. The doctrine of God's sovereignty does not lead to passivity in our lives. A Latin proverb puts it this way: "Providence assists not the idle."[8] There is no teaching in the Bible that removes our responsibility to act.

Let me introduce you to the doctrine of concurrence, which is a subset of the doctrine of God's providence. The doctrine of concurrence teaches that God is working *as* man is working. The word "concurrence" simply means "the simultaneous occurrence of events or circumstances."[9] As Louis Berkhof explains, the doctrine of divine occurrence "may be defined as the work of God by which He co-operates with all His creatures and causes them to act precisely as they do."[10] Both God and man are working at the same time. God is primary and man is secondary. But man is not passive in the process!

There is a beautiful balance in the Bible between the truths of God's sovereignty and man's responsibility. While God's providence was working in the life of Ruth (2:1), Ruth was responsible in going out to work in the field (2:3). God was working through the actions of Ruth to accomplish His purposes in her life. The doctrine of God's providence is not the same as fatalism.

John Maxwell tells the story of a man who was employed by a duke and duchess in Europe. He was called in to speak to his employer.

"James," said the duchess, "how long have you been with us?"

"About thirty years, Your Grace," he replied.

"As I recall, you were employed to look after the dog."

"Yes, Your Grace," James replied.

"James, that dog died twenty-seven years ago."

"Yes, Your Grace," said James. "What would you like me to do now?"

Maxwell comments, "Like James, too many people are waiting for someone else to tell them what to do next. Nearly all people have good thoughts, ideas, and intentions, but many of them never translate those into action. Doing so requires initiative."[11]

What responsibilities and opportunities do you have today? Take the initiative to develop a plan of action. Be encouraged through the bold actions of Ruth in this passage. God can work through your efforts to accomplish His purposes. As Oliver Cromwell said to his troops during the English Civil War, "Trust God and keep your powder dry."[12]

THE INCIDENTAL

So she set out and went and gleaned in the field after the reapers, and she happened to come to the part of the field belonging to Boaz, who was of the clan of Elimelech. (Ruth 2:3)

In this verse, we are introduced to the seemingly incidental coming of Ruth to the gleaner's field. This field curiously belongs to Boaz. At first reading, it appears to be a matter of mere good luck. But remember we were told earlier in the chapter that Boaz was a relative of Naomi through Elimelech (2:1). That detail was furnished to us so that we might theologically read into this apparently chance meeting.

We can infer that the hand of God was orchestrating this story. As John W. Reed observes, "The same providence that later led the magi to Bethlehem directed Ruth to the appropriate Bethlehem field."[13] There are no random encounters in the providence of God.

The reality of providence

This text is a masterpiece treatment on the subject of God's providence. Nothing just happens apart from the sovereign hand of God. Life might seem random but looks can be deceiving (2 Corinthians 5:7; Hebrews 11:1). The fact of God's providence must define the way we view our reality.

The Puritan Thomas Watson said, "There is no such thing as blind fate, but there is a Providence that guides and governs the world … Providence is God's ordering all issues and events of things, after the counsel of His will, to His own glory … The wheels in a clock seem to move contrary one to the other, but they help forward the motion of the clock."[14]

Another Puritan named Henry Law, who lived two centuries after Thomas Watson, wrote: "No sparrow falls, no leaf decays, but in accordance with God's ordering mind. Chance is a figment of a dreaming pillow. Chance never was and it never can be. Thus, to the child of God there is no trifle or unimportant event. Momentous issues often hang on quick words, on sudden looks, on unintended steps."[15]

Sinclair Ferguson encourages us to look at life like you would watch a split-screen television. On one side of the screen you might see chaos going on. On the other side of the screen, someone is giving you an interpretation of what's happening. He reflects on the story of Ruth in this way:

> Here then the author is helping us to view our lives as though they were being played out on a split screen on which we see both the sovereignty of God and his lordship over all the details of our lives, and also the contingency or unpredictability of the events of the world in which we live. From a human point of view, everything could be quite different from the way it is.
>
> Yet at the same time we recognize that in the midst of our confusion and happenstances and surprise of life there is a sovereign

> God in heaven whose hand is upon us every moment of the day,
> a God who reigns over every inch of the universe in which we lie.
> So we know that nothing "just happens ... "[16]

What great assurance this is! From our point of view, sorrow enters our lives and it all looks terrible. Things happen with no obvious explanation. We get a job opportunity from one company or rejected from another. Doors open and close for no apparent reason.

But on the other side of the split screen, God is working all things after the counsel of His will (Ephesians 1:11). God has a plan for your life. All of your days were written down in his book before you were even born (Psalm 139:16). God knows where you are going to live and work. God knows who your closest friends will be. God knows your children's names before they are even conceived. That's the reality of providence. Ferguson concludes from this truth: "That is why we can be quietly confident—not because we know exactly what God is doing in this unpredictable world, but because we know that what is unpredictable to us is already predicted by him."[17]

The realm of providence

This is a typical story in many ways. It could have been written a thousand times about other people. This is a story of marriage, grief, loss, and poverty. It's a story about unemployment, migration, and breaking into a new culture. There is love and a wedding and a nursery and happiness. It's just ordinary people living ordinary lives.

But providence has written this story, and that's what makes it so interesting. In the middle of it all, we're moving from the period of the judges to the establishment of a new king. This king will be named David and God will establish his throne. From David's line will come the King of kings, the Lord Jesus Christ. God is doing something remarkable in the midst of the mundane.

It's unlikely that any of us will ever witness a genuine miracle—an event in which God suspends the laws of nature. Louis Berkhof defines a miracle as "a supernatural work of God ... a work which is accomplished without the mediation of secondary causes."[18] When they are found in the Bible, miracles are usually connected with the giving of new revelation (Numbers 16:28; Jeremiah 32:20; John 2:11, 5:36).

When God performs a miracle, he suspends natural law. When God works in providence, he works through natural law. God's preferred method of establishing His kingdom is not one or two large miracles but thousands of interlocking providences played out in the lives of everyday people. The realm of God's providence is everyday life!

The English churchman Edward Pusey said this in the 19th century:

> This, then, is of faith, that everything, the very least, or what seems to us great, every change of the seasons, everything which touches us in mind, body, or estate, whether brought about through this outward senseless nature, or by the will of man, good or bad, is overruled to each of us by the all-holy and all-loving will of God.
>
> Whatever befalls us, however it befalls us, we must receive as the will of God. If it befalls us through man's negligence, or ill-will, or anger, still it is, in even the least circumstance, to us the will of God.
>
> For if the least thing could happen to us without God's permission, it would be something out of God's control. God's providence or His love would not be what they are. Almighty God Himself would not be the same God; not the God whom we believe, adore, and love.[19]

God is weaving life together in a marvelous way. Don't fall prey to discouragement. Don't become unbelieving in your thinking. Have a theological split screen before you at all times. Learn to walk by faith, not by sight.

The reach of providence

There are various facets to the reach of God's control over his creation. We notice the following in the story of Ruth and Naomi:

1. *Providence ordained the time of their arrival* (1:22). They arrived late spring or early summer and not during wintertime. This was during the beginning of the barley harvest. It was a good time to be back in Bethlehem.

2. *Providence ordained the provision for the poor* (2:2). God had a heart for the poor in Israel. He enacted a law to provide for them (Leviticus 19:9; Deuteronomy 24:19). Long before Ruth came onto the scene, God had made provision for her needs through the law in Israel. You might call this "preparatory providence."
3. *Providence ordained the right field* (2:3). In Israel, parcels of land ran into each other. There might have been boundary stones known to the owner alone, but there was nothing visible to distinguish which field belonged to which owner. It just so happened that Ruth entered the field of Boaz.

Remember, this was a time of rebellion in Israel. Not every farmer obeyed the law's provisions for the poor. Ruth could have entered other fields where she would have met a cruel master. But providence brought her to Boaz's field.

The tentacles of providence reach far and wide. Every moment in time falls under the umbrella of God's overruling providence. Though all human acts are free in the sense that they are self-determined, none are exempt from His overarching rule. God's providence is the real story behind our story. He is gracious and promises to do good to his people.

Jonathan Edwards observed:

> God's providence may not unfitly be compared to a large and long river, having innumerable branches beginning in different regions, and at a great distance one from another, and all conspiring to one common issue. After their very diverse and contrary courses which they hold for a while, yet all gathering more and more together the nearer they come to their common end, and all at length discharging themselves at one mouth into the same ocean.[20]

What a great statement! It is echoed by C.H. Spurgeon, who said, "We believe in a God of purposes and plans, who has not left a blind fate to tyrannize over the world, much less an aimless chance to rock it to and fro. We are not fatalists, neither are we doubters of providence and predestination."[21]

In 2009, I went home to Northern Ireland and met my friend, Eric Lindsay. Eric was a deacon at Great Victoria Street Baptist Church in Belfast. He told me that the year before, James Montgomery Boice had come to preach at the church. After preaching, he took an afternoon to trace his heritage in Northern Ireland. He started out by finding that the Boice family was connected to some pub, which wasn't very inspiring. Things got better when he discovered that his family was from a town called Tobermore and that he had one living relative. Boice said, tongue-in-cheek, "Eric, I'm really encouraged today because now I have both the luck of the Irish and the sovereignty of God going for me."

It was a humorous remark, not a theological statement. The truth is, friend, you don't need the luck of the Irish. You don't need chance or blind fate on your side because they don't exist. The sovereignty of God will take care of you. Divine providence will protect and guide you. We are the beneficiaries of a God who is eternally sovereign and wise. Each night, we can place our heads upon the pillow of God's providence. We can trust that He will be good to us in every season of life.

QUESTIONS FOR PERSONAL APPLICATION AND REFLECTION

1. The doctrine of providence teaches us that God controls every moment, every molecule and every movement within His creation. How does the doctrine of providence bring perspective to how you view your circumstances today?

2. Ruth 2:1 describes the character of Boaz as a "worthy man." The NIV translates this as "a man of outstanding character." What are some ways that men today can emulate Boaz's godly character?

3. The doctrine of God's sovereignty should never lead us to embrace the ideas of passivity or fatalism. Is there any area of life that you are especially prone to be passive in? How can you embrace your responsibility in this area?

4. Providence blesses initiative. Think through your own responsibilities and opportunities this day. What is one area of your life that you need to develop a plan of action for? What will be your plan of action?

5. Miracles are a suspension of natural laws where God intervenes in a demonstrable way. Yet there are no miracles in the book of Ruth. Why do you think believers might be prone to seek miraculous experiences? Take some time this week to thank God for His providence. Learn to rest your head on the pillow of God's sovereignty each night.

CHAPTER 5

FINDING FAVOR

RUTH 2:4–23

The English nonconformist pastor and preacher John Condor was born in 1714. The circumstances of his times were dark and foreboding. His grandfather Richard kissed young John on the forehead, and with tears in his eyes said: "Who knows what sad days these little eyes are likely to see?" At the end of his life and ministry, John Condor reflected on that incident from his childhood and remarked: "These eyes have for more than sixty years seen nothing but goodness and mercy follow me and the churches of Christ even to this day."[1]

I love that story and I think we all can identify with it. John's grandfather looked out and saw a discouraging future. But John experienced something far different. God showed him favor and blessed him in ways that his grandfather could not have imagined. As he looked back on his life, he didn't see half of the trouble that he had expected to see. He certainly came to know God's favor and kindness through difficult days.

It is a wonderful thing to find God's favor in tough times. God's kindness often allows us to beat the odds. Staring defeat and disaster in the face, many of us have come to know sustained victory. We can share in the confidence of David who said, "I believe that I shall look upon the goodness of the Lord in the land of the living!" (Psalm 27:13)

In Ruth Chapter 2, we are moving from the theme of *enduring sorrow* to *enjoying favor.* In Chapter 1, Ruth and Naomi returned home and faced a bleak future. In Chapter 2, the narrative turns a critical corner with the appearance of Boaz, "a worthy man" (2:1). The women begin to experience God's favor during difficult times (2:2, 10, 13). The focus of the story is shifting from Naomi's bitterness to God's blessing.

Warren Wiersbe once remarked, "If God is going to bless us, we have to be blessable."[2] It is an interesting statement. What he means is that although God's grace is unmerited and undeserved, there are attitudes and commitments that He promises to reward. We can't presume upon God's favor, but we can put ourselves in the way of it. Let's learn from Ruth how we can experience God's blessing.

RUTH'S REQUEST

*And behold, Boaz came from Bethlehem. And he said to the reapers, "The L*ORD *be with you!" And they answered, "The L*ORD *bless you." Then Boaz said to his young man who was in charge of the reapers, "Whose young woman is this?" And the servant who was in charge of the reapers answered, "She is the young Moabite woman, who came back with Naomi from the country of Moab. She said, 'Please let me glean and gather among the sheaves after the reapers.' So she came, and she has continued from early morning until now, except for a short rest." (Ruth 2:4–7)*

Ruth began her work while it was still morning. She believed that the early bird gets the worm. This was probably the morning after she and Naomi had arrived in Bethlehem, and they had returned "empty" (1:21). Ruth had no time to waste. With grit, determination and boldness, she set out to provide for herself and Naomi.

You have to love Ruth's "get up and go" spirit. To the young man who was in charge of the reapers, Ruth said: "Please let me glean and gather among the sheaves after the reapers" (2:7). There was no attitude of entitlement in her request. Her conduct was marked by tact and charm. She humbly expressed herself with wisdom and grace.

At the same time, this was a bold request! The law said that the poor could glean only around the edges of the field (Leviticus 19:9,

23:22). Ruth was asking to go beyond the requirements of the law. One commentator observes this was an "unusual request ... her choice reflects a holy boldness that was likely founded on her commitment to the Lord (1:16–17)."[3] Ruth was trusting in the generosity of the Lord's favor!

Ruth's example is instructive to us. She did the next best thing given the opportunities that were before her. Ecclesiastes 9:10 says, "Whatever your hand finds to do, do it with your might." It was the barley harvest, and the law allowed the poor to glean from the fields in Bethlehem. Ruth sized up the situation and worked with what she had. Instead of waiting for a miracle, she hustled at the door of opportunity. I love it!

Remember how Elisabeth Elliot said that life is often about doing "the next thing"?[4] Ruth did the next best thing and then the best thing after that. Her decisive steps led to the unfolding of a marvelous story. The man she meets in the field will become her husband, and they will have a child who will be the grandfather of David, from whose line will come the Messiah, the Savior of Israel. It will all happen because Ruth got up that morning and decided to go to work in the fields.

John Wooden is known as one of the greatest college basketball coaches of all time. He coached the UCLA basketball team to 10 national championships. Wooden provided this insight into his coaching philosophy: "When you improve a little each day, eventually big things occur ... Not tomorrow, not the next day, but eventually a big gain is made. Don't look for the quick, big improvement. Seek the small improvement one day at a time."[5]

That's a great perspective. Great things begin with taking small steps. Dear friend, this is practical theology for everyday life. The best thing that you and I can do—especially when we aren't sure what to do—is to *do the next thing that is before us.* Get moving! Get some momentum going in your life by taking the next step with the opportunities before you.

In 1994, my wife June and I moved to the United States from Northern Ireland. Stepping out in faith, we packed up our belongings and traveled with our three young daughters to a new country.

We arrived with no assurances of what the Lord would do. I enrolled as a student at The Master's Seminary, trusting God to provide for our needs. I remember listening to my mentor, John MacArthur, preach on Christian radio as I drove to my classes at seminary.

Since that day we set out for the States, the Lord has been gracious to our family in ways beyond what we could have asked or imagined. Today, I pastor a thriving church where the Word of God is honored. God has given me a radio ministry which ministers His Word across the country. By His grace we have been given favor, but it didn't happen overnight. It was a journey of decades. Looking back, I am convinced it has been the accumulation of small acts of faithfulness. In God's providence, our small steps of obedience can add up to something great.

In her classic devotional, *Streams in the Desert,* Lettie Cowman gives this paraphrase of Proverbs 4:12: "When thou goest, thy way shall be opened up before thee step by step." Cowman comments, "The love of God quite as often withholds the view of the entire distance of the winding path through life. He reveals it to us step by step and from corner to corner. Hence it is necessary to trust Him to lead, for He can see around the bend in the road. He knows what lies ahead, and whether we can cope with the situation now or later. He consults our wants, not our wishes, like a wise and loving Father. His corners are not the end of the way."[6]

Dear friend, are you rounding a corner in life? Be encouraged that the Lord leads us step by step on the journey. As you take the next step of obedience, the path will open up before you. May the Lord's kind providence multiply the fruits of your labor.

RUTH'S RECOGNITION

And behold, Boaz came from Bethlehem. And he said to the reapers, "The Lord be with you!" And they answered, "The Lord bless you" Then Boaz said to his young man who was in charge of the reapers, "Whose young woman is this?" (Ruth 2:4–5)

The word "behold" (1:4) is emphatic and calls the reader to take notice of the next event. The meeting of Ruth and Boaz is the turning point in this story. Ruth catches the attention of Boaz, who has arrived to check on the work in his field. In this pivotal moment in the book of Ruth, we see the twin themes of God's providence and Ruth's presence.

God's providence

It was more than coincidence that Boaz happened to arrive that day to inspect his field. The meeting was flawlessly orchestrated by the hand of God and perfectly timed to achieve His purposes. Observe the gracious greeting of Boaz to his workers: "The Lord be with you!" Boaz shows himself to be a godly man living in an ungodly generation.

It is amazing to consider how often God intervenes in the lives of his servants. Let's look at a few examples from the Old Testament:

- The infant Moses' intersection with Pharaoh's daughter on the Nile positioned him to eventually set God's people free.
- Abigail offered David's army some food just in time to stop a rampage on her home. Abigail's foolish husband later died, and she became the king's wife.
- When Queen Esther's husband couldn't sleep and asked for something to read, he was brought the book of history, and he heard the account of Mordecai saving him. This eventually led to the Israelites' empowerment to defend themselves against their enemies and escape annihilation.[7]

Ruth gleaned in the field and was brought into the genealogy of Jesus Christ! God is always working. There are no random events. What seems like coincidence is really His providence. Take a look at your own life's circumstances in light of God's sovereignty and grace. Trust that He is working in the midst of your life story.

In 1874, the great English Baptist pastor F.B. Meyer had come to the end of his ministry at Victoria Road Baptist Church in Leicester.

He was an evangelist and a soul-winner, but this was a traditional church that wanted a "proper pastor." Meyer had upset the congregation and realized it was not a good marriage. He resigned and accepted a call to pastor a church in another city. On the way to the post office to send his letter of acceptance, Meyer bumped into a friend named Arthur Rust. Rust was the brother-in-law of W.Y. Fullerton, a famous evangelist who worked alongside C.H. Spurgeon.

Meyer was telling his friend about the new pastorate. But Rust told Meyer that before he accepted the call, he should hear about an emerging young congregation in Leicester. It was filled with young men and women. The fellowship was dynamic and gospel-centered. There were several young businessmen in it who would bankroll the pastor's wages. Fullerton told Meyer that he should inquire about it.

Meyer ripped up his letter of acceptance, and ultimately became part of forming the church known as Melbourne Hall. This church would go on to have a very fruitful ministry and impact many lives for the cause of Christ. How different things would have been if Meyer had not run into his friend on the way to the post office. What looked like a chance encounter turned out to be a divine appointment made by the providence of God.[8]

You never know whom you are going to bump into and how that might change your life! God brings events and people into our lives to influence us and direct us onto the right path. He governs the details of our lives in order to bring about the greatest good for His people. The Lord is always doing something in us and for us (Romans 8:28).

Ruth's presence

While the theme of God's providence is central in this story, it's important that we also see Ruth's presence. We observe that Ruth simply showed up for work that day! That fact may seem obvious, but consider the alternatives. What if Ruth had slept in? What if she had procrastinated in going out to the field? What if Boaz had arrived to find the field empty? The narrative would have told a much different story.

I want you to appreciate the fact that Ruth was in the field for that crucial meeting. God's providence was working concurrently with Ruth's responsible behavior. In sum, Ruth showed up. Boaz showed up. And on that day, God showed up in a wonderful way!

Dear friend, don't underestimate the power of simply being present. Missed days in the Christian life are a certain kind of tragedy. The physicist Stephen Hawking once said, "Half the battle is just showing up." Remarking on the key to success, Thomas Edison said "genius is ... ninety-nine percent perspiration." There is no substitute for consistently being where you should be in life.

Leroy "Satchel" Paige was one of the greats in the world of baseball. History remembers him as the first black player to pitch in the World Series. Folklore tells us that he won 2,100 games, 60 in one season, and 55 without giving up a hit. And that was before he was allowed in the majors as a 42-year old "rookie" pitching for the Cleveland Indians. Everything about the man was memorialized, including his famous sayings. One of his best sayings goes like this: "You win a few, you lose a few. Some get rained out. But you got to dress for all of them."[9]

There's a lot of wisdom in that statement! No matter how we feel on a given day, we have to get up, dress up and show up. Part of a winning strategy in life involves just being present. Ruth showed up in time for a pivotal meeting, and things began to look up for her and Naomi. What a difference a day can make—in your life and mine as well. What a great motivation to show up and get to work each day!

RUTH'S REAPING

> *She said, 'Please let me glean and gather among the sheaves after the reapers.' So she came, and she has continued from early morning until now, except for a short rest." (Ruth 2:7)*

Gleaning in the fields was backbreaking work. Ruth diligently labored from early morning until evening, with dirt under her fingernails and sweat on her brow (2:7, 17). She had a great work ethic, and God blessed her for it.

It's a simple thought but it needs repeating: in a day of growing laziness and an attitude of entitlement, God blesses those who are hard at work. There is dignity in fulfilling the responsibilities of everyday labor. God will bless you for your punctuality and service.

This is great encouragement for anyone who labors in an assembly line, in an office, in a store or in the field: *our work matters to God*. Old Testament scholar Daniel Block observes that in the narrative of Ruth, there is a theology of work being presented that focuses on these points:

1. *Food is God's gracious gift in response to human effort* (2:17). We need to pray for God to give us our daily bread, but we also must roll up our sleeves and work for it.
2. *Work is an expression of commitment to the well-being of the family* (2:2–3, 1:16–17). Ruth had no husband, so she set out to provide. She was committed to Naomi and expressed her love in action.
3. *The workplace is an environment in which to demonstrate the fear of God* (2:4). Boaz shows a fear of God before his workers. He treats the foreigner with respect. The Bible is not uncaring regarding the plight of women in the ancient world.[10]

By implication, this narrative is a warning against the sins of sloth and laziness (Proverbs 6:9–11, 10:45, 18:9, 20:4, 26:14). Perhaps you have heard the story of the college student who was trying to decide whether he should study. He grabbed a coin, flipped it, and in midair said, "Heads, I'm going to the movies; tails, I'm going to watch TV; if it stands on its edge, I'm going to study." Some sluggards are too lazy to even flip the coin![11]

Don't be the sluggard who always thinks about the prospect of work but never gets down to doing the job. The biblical principle is that we will reap what we sow (Galatians 6:6–10). Ruth reminds us of the dignity and value of work.

RUTH'S REPUTATION

Then Boaz said to Ruth, "Now, listen, my daughter, do not go to glean in another field or leave this one, but keep close to my young women. Let your eyes be on the field that they are reaping, and go after them. Have I not charged the young men not to touch you? And when you are thirsty, go to the vessels and drink what the young men have drawn." Then she fell on her face, bowing to the ground, and said to him, "Why have I found favor in your eyes, that you should take notice of me, since I am a foreigner?" But Boaz answered her, "All that you have done for your mother-in-law since the death of your husband has been fully told to me, and how you left your father and mother and your native land and came to a people that you did not know before. (Ruth 2:8–11)

Naomi and Ruth were the talk of the town (1:19). Boaz had not escaped the buzz and was fully informed about the excellent reputation of this foreigner. He says to Ruth, "All that you have done … has been fully told to me" (2:11). In the swirl of gossip, Ruth had gained a reputation of grit and goodness that made her a bit of a folk hero.

We are reminded that reputation is precious and character is priceless. Proverbs 22:1 says, "A good name is to be chosen rather than great riches, and favor is better than silver or gold." Notice that there is no physical description of Ruth in this book. Ruth is not defined by the appearance of her body or the complexion of her skin. We are not told if she is tall or short, plump or skinny. We know nothing about that because, in the end, it doesn't matter. Ruth is known for her godliness and loyalty. Proverbs 31:30 says, "Charm is deceitful, and beauty is vain, but a woman who fears the Lord is to be praised."

Ruth gained a reputation as "a woman of noble character" (3:11, NIV). William Hershey Davis once said, "Your character is what God knows you to be. Your reputation is what men think you are."[12] That's a good distinction, and yet the two can be related. D.L. Moody once remarked, "If I take care of my character, my reputation will take care of itself."[13] There is an undeniable power to godly character.

RUTH'S REFUGE

The LORD repay you for what you have done, and a full reward be given you by the LORD, the God of Israel, under whose wings you have come to take refuge!" (Ruth 2:12)

Boaz articulates his hope that God will honor and bless Ruth's life. Ruth's trust in God is beautifully described as taking refuge under His wings (Psalm 36:7; 91:1–2, 4). This is a warm and wonderful picture of a mother hen brooding over her offspring. It can also be portrayed as an eagle teaching a little eaglet how to fly (Exodus 19:4; Deuteronomy 32:11–12). As Joel Gregory has well said, "The God whom we meet in Christ not only promises us a hiding place but He promises to stabilize us like an eagle with its eaglet."[14]

God has promised to care for His people. This truth has reassured the saints of God throughout church history. In 1892, after a year of intensive work in Great Britain, D.L. Moody sailed for home, eager to get back to his family and his work. The ship left Southampton amid many farewells. After three days at sea, the ship ground to a halt with a broken shaft; before long, it began to take water. Needless to say, the crew and passengers were desperate because nobody knew of any rescue ships in the area. After two anxiety-filled days, Moody asked for permission to hold a meeting, and—to his surprise—nearly every passenger attended. He opened his Bible to Psalm 91 and, holding onto a pillar to steady himself, he read: "He that dwelleth in the secret place of the Most High shall abide under the shadow of the Almighty."

Moody wrote later, "It was the darkest hour of my life … relief came in prayer. God heard my cry, and enabled me to say, from the depth of my soul, 'Thy will be done.' I went to bed and fell asleep almost immediately …" God answered prayer and saved the ship, sending another vessel to tow it to port. Psalm 91 became a vibrant, new scripture to D.L. Moody and he discovered that the safest place in the world is in the shadow of the Almighty, "under His wings."[15]

You and I must discover this truth as well. Ruth and her mother-in-law were penniless and faced an uncertain future, but Ruth had taken refuge in God. In the rest of the story, we see that the Lord will lift up these two widows and carry them on eagles' wings. Isaiah 40:31 says, "they who wait for the LORD shall renew their strength; they shall mount up with wings like eagles; they shall run and not be weary; they shall walk and not faint." God is willing to shelter us under His wings.

RUTH'S RETURN

And at mealtime Boaz said to her, "Come here and eat some bread and dip your morsel in the wine." So she sat beside the reapers, and he passed to her roasted grain. And she ate until she was satisfied, and she had some left over. When she rose to glean, Boaz instructed his young men, saying, "Let her glean even among the sheaves, and do not reproach her. And also pull out some from the bundles for her and leave it for her to glean, and do not rebuke her." So she gleaned in the field until evening. Then she beat out what she had gleaned, and it was about an ephah of barley. And she took it up and went into the city. (Ruth 2:14–18a)

This was a good day of labor for Ruth. It produced an ephah of barley. Paul Miller observes that "an ephah is about twenty-two liters, enough food for one person for at least half a month."[16] Ruth had plenty of food to take home. She shares a meal with Boaz and then returns to Naomi.

Her mother-in-law saw what she had gleaned. She also brought out and gave her what food she had left over after being satisfied. And her mother-in-law said to her, "Where did you glean today? And where have you worked? Blessed be the man who took notice of you." So she told her mother-in-law with whom she had worked and said, "The man's name with whom I worked today is Boaz." And Naomi said to her daughter-in-law, "May he be blessed by the LORD, whose kindness has not forsaken the living or the dead!" (Ruth 2:18b–20a)

For the first time in the story, Naomi's attitude starts to change. There is excitement in her reaction as she realizes that Boaz is a relative of Elimelech (2:1). Her spirits are lifted. Her hopes are revived. Miss Pleasant ("Naomi")—who had become Miss Unpleasant ("Mara")—is singing and smiling once again. She has been wrong in her assessment of God's dealings. God is not against her as she supposed!

How kind God is to Naomi! Allow her story to encourage you today. Dale Ralph Davis recounts how the focus returns to Naomi at the end of every chapter.

- Chapter 1 ends with Naomi being given *Ruth's companionship* (1:19–22).
- Chapter 2 ends with Naomi being given *barley for food* (2:20–23).
- Chapter 3 ends with Naomi being given *hope for Ruth's marriage* (3:16–18).
- Chapter 4 ends with Naomi being given *a grandchild* (4:13–17).[17]

Every chapter ends with some resolution of a problem in Naomi's life! The literary pattern of this text is saying that God is preoccupied with Naomi's welfare. He has not left her nor forsaken her. God is showing His *hesed* to Naomi.

Initial impressions can be wrong. We can sometimes misread a situation and make misguided conclusions. I remember reading a story about Israeli stateswoman Golda Meir, who came to the United States in 1948 to raise funds for the Israeli Defense Forces (IDF). She had been quite successful in raising money for this important Jewish cause. One night in Palm Beach, Florida, she spoke before a gathering of well-heeled Americans decked in furs and jewels. As she sipped her coffee and looked around the room, she grew discouraged by a crowd that didn't seem interested in hearing about suffering and death in Israel. Nevertheless, she bit her tongue, held her temper, and got up to speak. By the end of that night, she raised 1.5 million dollars—enough to buy a winter coat for every IDF soldier.[18]

We can all hastily conclude that a certain situation is hopeless. But if we have patience to follow a story to the end, we may be surprised at the good that is accomplished. Naomi's story looked like it was over when her husband and sons died. But God was not finished with her.

RUTH'S REDEEMER

Naomi also said to her, "The man is a close relative of ours, one of our redeemers." And Ruth the Moabite said, "Besides, he said to me, 'You shall keep close by my young men until they have finished all my harvest.'" And Naomi said to Ruth, her daughter-in-law, "It is good, my daughter, that you go out with his young women, lest in another field you be assaulted." (Ruth 2:20b–22)

The Hebrew term for "redeemer" is *goel*. A *goel* is someone who, under the law of God, could redeem a family who was in trouble. A redeemer could avenge a murder, pay off a debt, or marry the wife of a deceased relative in order to carry the family name forward.

We know that the greatest redeemer of all is God's Son, Jesus Christ. Ephesians 1:7 says, "In him we have redemption through his blood." Jesus purchased for us an eternal redemption. But in the Bible, there are also human redeemers. These are people in a position of strength who must fulfill an obligation to assist those in need. Naomi wonders if Boaz will be such a redeemer. We will see in Chapter 4 that he fulfills that role.

The fact is, we all need human redeemers. We are all in relationship with one another. We have responsibilities toward each other. Fathers have material obligations, married couples have sexual obligations. Elders have pastoral obligations. Neighbors have societal obligations. Governments have legal obligations. Children have parental obligations. Christians have evangelical obligations.

People are depending on us. If we don't come through, they won't make it through. If we don't stand by our obligations, they will fall down. You may not fulfill the *goel* calling of the Israelite man, but God has put people under you and around you. You have an obligation and responsibility to bless them and help them.

You hear a lot today about the Bill of Rights. Our Constitution is *par excellence*, the greatest in the world. It offers to United States citizens the greatest freedoms and calls us to aspire to the greatest kind of life. We love that. As Americans, we should be proud of the Constitution. But if our founders perhaps made one mistake, it's that along with the Bill of Rights they should have also written a Bill of Responsibilities. When we emphasize rights without also teaching responsibilities, we keep people from being all that God has called them to be.

Before God, we are responsible for one another. This reminds me of a very interesting court case in Massachusetts back in 1928. It concerned a man who had been walking on a boat dock when he suddenly tripped over a rope and fell into the cold, deep water of the bay. He came up sputtering and yelling for help and then sank again, obviously in trouble. His friends were too far away to get to him, but on another dock a few yards away was a young man sprawled on a deck chair, sunbathing. "Help, I can't swim!" came the desperate shout. The young man, an excellent swimmer, only turned his head to watch as the man floundered in the water, sank, came up sputtering again in total panic, and then disappeared forever.

The family of the drowned man was so upset by that display of callous indifference that they sued the sunbather. They lost. The court reluctantly ruled that the man on the dock had no legal responsibility to try to save the other man's life. In effect, the law agreed with Cain: I am not my brother's keeper, and I have every right to mind my own business and refuse to involve myself in others' lives.[19]

While indifference may be legal, the Bible considers it immoral. To refuse to meet the urgent needs of others is plainly sinful. The truth is, we are our brother's keeper. It has been well said: "The thing that keeps your feet on the ground is the responsibility placed on your shoulders."[20] Boaz was a human redeemer who fulfilled his obligation to care for those in need. In this way, his life pointed to the ultimate Redeemer, the God-man Jesus Christ. Paul Miller writes, "Our lives should reflect the redeeming life of Jesus. If that were to happen, we would live not one life, but a thousand lives." May God grant us a full life of caring for others. May God grant us to experience His kindness and favor!

QUESTIONS FOR PERSONAL APPLICATION AND REFLECTION

1. Review the two requests of Ruth in Ruth 2:2 and Ruth 2:7. What were the dangers Ruth would have faced by taking initiative in this way? What does this type of initiative tell us about Ruth's character and attitude?

2. D.L. Moody said, "If I take care of my character, my reputation will take care of itself." In Ruth 2:1, Boaz is called "a worthy man" (ESV) or "a man of great wealth" (NKJV). In Ruth 3:11, Ruth is called a "virtuous woman" (NKJV) or "a woman of excellence" (NASB). Why are examples like Boaz and Ruth so needed for men and women in the church today? Women: How would you use the narrative of Ruth to disciple a younger woman in the faith? Men: How would you use the example of Boaz to encourage younger men to pursue spiritual excellence?

3. At the end of each chapter, the book of Ruth keeps coming back to a focus on Naomi. What is the progression of Naomi's experience through the book of Ruth? Why do you think that each chapter ends with a focus on Naomi?

4. We are called to be human redeemers to those in society who are in need. Who do you have a responsibility to bless and help today? How can you faithfully fulfill that responsibility?

5. Ruth's trust in God is described as taking refuge under His wings (Ruth 2:12). In what situations of life have you found it necessary to take refuge under the Lord's wings? How does this picture speak comfort to your soul?

CHAPTER 6

COLD FEET

RUTH 3:1-18

In his book entitled *Being Single and Satisfied,* Dr. Tony Evans tells of a single woman who was in deep discussion with her pastor one day about the subject of marriage. The pastor said, "You know, God has designed the perfect plan for marriage: one man and one woman together for life. You cannot improve upon God's plan." The single woman looked at the pastor and replied, "Pastor, I don't want to improve on it. I just want to get in on it."[1]

Getting in on God's perfect plan for marriage is sometimes easier said than done. Many singles feel as if their lives are in a holding pattern—like an airplane that is supposed to be landing at its destination but has been ordered to circle the airport. The Bible shares some interesting ways that singles have gotten in on God's perfect plan for marriage. Deuteronomy 25:5–10 describes the concept of levirate marriage, where a relative marries a widow in order to produce an heir to carry on the family line. With this concept in mind, let's pick up the story of Ruth and Boaz in Chapter 3. We'll see how their relationship moves towards marriage under Naomi's guidance.

THE PLAN

Then Naomi her mother-in-law said to her, "My daughter, should I not seek rest for you, that it may be well with you? Is not Boaz our relative, with whose young women you were? See, he is winnowing barley tonight

> *at the threshing floor. Wash therefore and anoint yourself, and put on your cloak and go down to the threshing floor, but do not make yourself known to the man until he has finished eating and drinking. But when he lies down, observe the place where he lies. Then go and uncover his feet and lie down, and he will tell you what to do." And she replied, "All that you say I will do." (Ruth 3:1–5)*

It's been said that there are four kinds of people in the world: those who make things happen, those who watch things happen, those who wonder what has happened, and those who don't know that anything happened.[2] Naomi is the kind of person who makes things happen! As we open Chapter 3, the harvest season is done. The crops have been gathered in. The wheat has been separated from the chaff. It's time to celebrate! The famine is over.

Ruth's introduction to Boaz was a game-changing event. The future looked brighter as soon as the women found out that Boaz was a close relative who could fulfill the role of a kinsman-redeemer. A marriage between Ruth and Boaz would restore the family estate, perpetuate the name of Elimelech through an heir, and provide security to Ruth as a young widow. Naomi hears wedding bells in the not-so-distant future. She wants to see Ruth settled in life.

But now Naomi is a little concerned. She likely thought that the interest Boaz had shown in Ruth would have blossomed into something more substantial by this time. Bible scholar R.L. Hubbard comments, "This chapter relates the climactic turning point of the entire story. Indeed, there is no higher level of dramatic tension and suspense than here."[3] At this crucial moment, Naomi plays the role of matchmaker and helps move Ruth and Boaz toward marriage!

Naomi's plan was brilliant

It seems that Boaz needed a push, a nudge in the right direction. Naomi implemented a well-thought-out plan, leaving nothing to chance. Her plan was grounded in wisdom and careful reflection. Paul Miller writes, "Thinking, planning, and problem solving are completely intertwined with romance, love, and audacity ... It's good to think in love even as you are falling in love."[4]

In the movie, *The Iron Lady,* actress Meryl Streep plays the role of the English Prime Minister Margaret Thatcher. At one point in the movie, Thatcher is asked how she is feeling. She replies, "One of the great problems of our age is that we are governed by people who care more about feelings than they do about thoughts and ideas. Thoughts and ideas. That interests me. Ask me what I'm thinking."[5]

Love thinks and plans as much as it feels. Naomi had done her homework in terms of the details of how she was going to encourage this relationship. She directs Ruth to meet Boaz at the threshing floor and to lie down at his feet. This was most likely a symbolic proposal of marriage.[6]

Naomi's plan was brave

Although it was well thought-out, the plan called for a good deal of courage. Ruth would have to go to the other side of town, in the dark, to meet Boaz. The threshing floor was sometimes associated with prostitution (Hosea 9:1). Ruth could have been a victim of mischief or abuse. What if she were seen in the company of Boaz by those who didn't understand the purity of the situation? This could lead to scandal and ruined reputations.

Would Boaz accept or reject the advance of this foreigner? The outcome certainly was not guaranteed. It was a step of faith. These women were trusting God and also banking on Boaz, a man of godly character. Naomi and Ruth planned and entrusted themselves to the providence of God. Their actions were certainly not reckless, but they were risky!

My friend, I don't know where you're at in life. I don't know where you are in terms of relationships, marriage, or business. You may be at a crossroads and looking at a situation that has inherent risks to it. But if you're willing to discern the will of God and live for His glory, you'll be up for the challenge. I would say, go for it! Be in the category of people who make things happen.

When June and I left the pastorate of a Baptist church in Northern Ireland in 1994 to move to America, we felt God calling us to enroll at

The Master's Seminary. Dr. John MacArthur, whom we had admired and esteemed from a distance, had invited us to come out to the school. We decided to take the plunge and move to California.

It was a big risk. In fact, June hadn't even been to the United States before. But God was good and He provided. He gave us dear friends who graciously supported us financially. Looking back now on the journey, we see the providence of God unfolding.

But on the other side of the pond, with three little girls, leaving financial security and all that we knew, it was not an easy decision. At that time, I remember reading: "You will never see or seek new horizons unless you are willing to lose sight of the shore."[7]

Dear friends, let's not settle and become too comfortable. Let's be willing to take risks for the gospel of Jesus Christ. Let's trust that the Lord will work in us and for us. He will show Himself to be faithful in our lives.

Naomi's plan was balanced

Charles Spurgeon was asked how he reconciled the truths of divine sovereignty and human responsibility. He asked, "I never reconcile two friends."[8] Ruth and Naomi's story highlights the balance between praying and taking action. These ladies confessed their belief in the providence of God, but they weren't reduced to twiddling their thumbs. Their understanding of God's character and provision led them to take bold action!

In Scripture, we find the happy marriage of planning and providence:

- Boaz prays for Ruth to be blessed (2:12) and will be challenged to answer his own prayer (3:9).
- Nehemiah prays and plans and then acts by asking the king to rebuild the walls of Jerusalem (Nehemiah 2:1–8).
- Jesus said, "My Father is working until now, and I am working" (John 5:17).

Once asked if he was a Calvinist, John Newton plopped a sugar cube into his tea, stirred the hot liquid, and said, "I am more of a

Calvinist than anything else; but I use my Calvinism in my writing and preaching as I use this sugar. I do not give it alone, and whole; but mixed, and diluted ... I think these doctrines should be in a sermon like sugar in a dish of tea, which sweetens every drop, but is nowhere to be found in a lump—tasted everywhere, though prominent nowhere."[9]

Our understanding of the sovereignty of God should be balanced with our embrace of man's responsibility. The providence of God does not make us passive. May this wonderful balance be found in our lives as well!

THE PROPOSAL

So she went down to the threshing floor and did just as her mother-in-law had commanded her. And when Boaz had eaten and drunk, and his heart was merry, he went to lie down at the end of the heap of grain. Then she came softly and uncovered his feet and lay down. (Ruth 3:6–7)

Out of submission to her mother-in-law, Ruth goes down to the threshing floor and carries out the plan with precision. Boaz has worked all day and is guarding the harvest. He's in a good place. The harvest is complete, and he and his friends are feasting and celebrating a job well done. His belly is full, his mood is happy, and it's time for a little siesta.

Boaz lies down to sleep and Ruth comes out of the shadows. She lies at his feet and uncovers them (3:7). There's a lot of talk among the commentators about Ruth's action. Was it something sexual or inappropriate? The uncovering of the feet can be a euphemism for a sexual encounter. Many commentators of a liberal stripe cast this scene as an act of seduction. But is it?

No, don't believe that for a second! The great Bible teacher and professor Dr. Jim Rosscup strongly held to the view that there is no impropriety in this narrative. He passed along to me his handwritten thoughts on why this is true:

- Boaz is a man of character (3:2).

- Ruth is obeying, not disobeying her mother-in-law. She is acting out of good faith (3:5).
- There can be a simple uncovering of the feet. This is the simple, plain reading of the text (3:7).
- Ruth is called a woman of excellence (3:11) and acts in accordance with her character.
- Boaz is willing to be a *goel,* a redeemer. He is not going to take advantage of Ruth (3:11).
- Boaz invokes the Lord's name—"as the LORD lives, I will redeem you" (3:13).
- When there is something sexually inappropriate in the text, the text usually tells you that.[10]

It has been well said, "when the plain sense of Scripture makes common sense, seek no other sense."[11] Ruth simply uncovered Boaz's feet. We should read nothing more into that statement. There's no sexual immorality; it's all above board. When the wind blew, Boaz woke up. To his shock and surprise, he found Ruth at his feet.

> *At midnight the man was startled and turned over, and behold, a woman lay at his feet! He said, "Who are you?" And she answered, "I am Ruth, your servant. Spread your wings over your servant, for you are a redeemer." And he said, "May you be blessed by the LORD, my daughter. You have made this last kindness greater than the first in that you have not gone after young men, whether poor or rich. And now, my daughter, do not fear. I will do for you all that you ask, for all my fellow townsmen know that you are a worthy woman. And now it is true that I am a redeemer. Yet there is a redeemer nearer than I. Remain tonight, and in the morning, if he will redeem you, good; let him do it. But if he is not willing to redeem you, then, as the LORD lives, I will redeem you. Lie down until the morning." So she lay at his feet until the morning, but arose before one could recognize another. And he said, "Let it not be known that the woman came to the threshing floor." And when she came to her mother-in-law, she said, "How did you fare, my daughter?" Then she told her all that the man had done for her, saying, "These six measures of barley he gave to me, for he said to me, 'You must not*

go back empty-handed to your mother-in-law.'" She replied, "Wait, my daughter, until you learn how the matter turns out, for the man will not rest but will settle the matter today." (Ruth 3:8–18)

Boaz notes that there is a complication. There is another near relative, and he has first dibs. But if he would not do it, Boaz assured Ruth that he would be happy to redeem her. He guards her reputation: Ruth leaves early in the morning while it's still dark and gets home with some grain for Naomi.

The chapter ends on a cliffhanger. Boaz goes off to talk to his relative. But since Chapter 3 records Boaz's unofficial marriage proposal, let's consider what we can learn so far about dating and marriage. Here are some abiding principles from the text that speak into our day and context.

The love expressed

The church father Augustine defined virtue as a rightly ordered love.[12] What he meant was that the Christian's primary love should be for God Himself. Every lesser love should be submitted to the greater love. The lesser love will blossom and grow when it finds its proper place.

The love between Boaz and Ruth was ordered in this way. It was a relationship that put the needs of others first. It's not that there was no genuine affection or attraction between these two, but their love wasn't dominated by a self-indulgent emotion. Ruth kept her responsibilities to Naomi and the family of Elimelech. In like manner, Boaz fulfilled his duty to Ruth and the law of Moses. Their love was rightly ordered and their relationship was blessed. What a great example for Christians today!

In our society, this type of love seems strange because we have largely romanticized the concept of love. We have individualized love to our detriment. I don't believe that the concept of arranged marriage needs to be an abiding pattern. But I do believe that our love for each other needs to be subject to the greater love—for God and neighbor. Did you notice that this is as much a love story between

Ruth and Naomi as it is a love story between Boaz and Ruth? As C.S. Lewis has well said, "When I have learnt to love God better than my earthly dearest, I shall love my earthly dearest better than I do now."[13]

I once spoke at a pastoral installation service, and at the celebration dinner the night before the installation, the pastor's father-in-law shared how thrilled he was to see where this couple was in life. He said it was a father's dream come true. He had prayed that God would give his daughter a man who loved God more than he loved her. That's a wonderful prayer of a father who loved his daughter with discernment. Boaz and Ruth knew this type of rightly ordered love! They loved each other most because they loved God first.

The lives expressed

Remember how Boaz describes Ruth as "a woman of excellence"?[14] This is the same type of language used to describe the excellent wife in Proverbs 31:10–31. In the Hebrew Bible, the book of Ruth comes after the book of Proverbs. Ruth is an illustration of the woman of excellence in Proverbs 31.

We don't get any physical descriptions of Ruth or Boaz. Rather, the couple is marked by faith in God and obedience to Scripture. Their relationship is based on the covenant love of God. If you think about it, Ruth and Boaz didn't have much in common from an earthly perspective. As my friend Stephen Davey observes:

- one was rich, the other was poor;
- one was a business owner, the other a migrant worker;
- one was single, the other had been married;
- one had experienced the death of a spouse, the other hadn't;
- one was a mature believer, the other a new believer;
- one was financially independent; the other lived hand-to-mouth.[15]

Yet their relationship was a match made in heaven! Young people, as you seek a spouse, let your pursuit be based on character, not charisma. Make your pursuit about Christlikeness, not physical appearance. Remember that "charm is deceitful and beauty is vain" (Proverbs 31:30). Real compatibility in marriage comes from a common love for God.

The language expressed

Ruth and Boaz's courtship is marked by the language of commitment. The wording used in this passage is covenantal in nature. Boaz uses the phrase, "As the LORD lives" (3:13), which is the Old Testament expression of making a solemn vow. In this chapter, Ruth keeps her promise to Naomi. In turn, Boaz makes a promise to Ruth before God.

Fundamentally, marriage is a promise kept. The language of the Old Testament regarding marriage is one of covenant (Malachi 2:14; Proverbs 2:14; Ezekiel 16:8). Marriage is not a convention or a convenience but a solemn promise made before God.

In 2004, Robertson McQuilkin wrote an article entitled "Living by Vows" in the magazine *Christianity Today*. He wrote about his wife's struggle with Alzheimer's disease and his decision to step down as the President of Columbia Bible College and Seminary. He explained:

> The decision was made, in a way, 42 years ago when I promised to care for Muriel "in sickness and in health ... till death do us part." So, as I told the students and faculty, as a man of my word, integrity has something to do with it. But so does fairness. She has cared for me fully and sacrificially all these years; if I cared for her for the next 40 years I would not be out of her debt. ...
>
> I love Muriel. She is a delight to me—her childlike dependence and confidence in me, her warm love, occasional flashes of that wit I used to relish so, her happy spirit and tough resilience in the face of her continual distressing frustration. I don't have to care for her. I get to! It is a high honor to care for so wonderful a person.[16]

McQuilkin understood that marriage is a covenant worth keeping. He was faithful to his promise in sickness and in health. What a great testimony to the binding nature of the marital vows! When we keep the covenant, the covenant keeps us.

THE PAUSE

And he said, "Bring the garment you are wearing and hold it out." So she held it, and he measured out six measures of barley and put it on her. Then she went into the city. And when she came to her mother-in-law, she said, "How did you fare, my daughter?" Then she told her all that the man had done for her, saying, "These six measures of barley he gave to me, for he said to me, 'You must not go back empty-handed to your mother-in-law.'" She replied, "Wait, my daughter, until you learn how the matter turns out, for the man will not rest but will settle the matter today." (Ruth 3:15–18)

Ruth doesn't return empty-handed to Naomi. Boaz pours six measures of barley into Ruth's shawl. While the provision of barley is a small expression of kindness, it is a reminder of God's care and faithfulness for these two women. In addition, the barley was most likely foreshadowing a fuller harvest to come in the marriage of Boaz to Ruth. Small tokens of God's kindness and provision can be a trail of crumbs that lead to a larger feast! We are wise to recount every blessing from the Lord, no matter how small.

The chapter ends with the fact that there was nothing more that the women could do but see how the matter might turn out. They didn't know the outcome, but they knew that Boaz would keep his word and not rest until he had an answer one way or another. Up until this point in the story, Ruth had been the one taking initiative and driving the story forward. Now she is in the position of patiently waiting for another to act on her behalf.

At times, God calls us to boldly act, to be courageous and to take risks in life. At other times, God calls us to patiently wait and to leave the matter in His hands. Alistair Begg has wisely observed, "Waiting is a part of life—our physical and spiritual life. We wait for God to intervene in our situation, to answer prayers, to fulfill his purposes and for Jesus to return ... like Boaz and Ruth, you have no idea what God is doing behind the scenes and what part your waiting will play in God's plan of salvation."[17] It's not easy to sit still and wait for the acceptance letter, the job offer, the pregnancy test, or the answer to prayer. Yet God teaches us many lessons while we wait on His timing.

The famous missionary Dr. Hudson Taylor often shared his burden for China with church groups. Many young people expressed an interest in joining his ministry. But years in China had taught Taylor what a Christian's witness there required. He wisely warned the eager volunteers that there were three absolutely indispensable requirements for a missionary: 1. Patience 2. Patience 3. Patience.[18]

In seasons of waiting, we are prone to become restless and impatient. But listen to the counsel of Warren Wiersbe: "Horses are prone to rush ahead and mules often insist on being stubborn. When we walk by faith, we dare not make either of these mistakes or we will be embarrassed and get detoured. Waiting on the Lord is not wasted time; it is invested time as we stay out of God's way until He gives us the signal to act. God is not in a hurry!"[19]

Dear friend, are you sitting today in the waiting room of life? Hear the encouragement of the Scriptures:

- "Wait for the Lord; be strong, and let your heart take courage; wait for the Lord!" (Psalm 27:14)
- "… they who wait for the Lord shall renew their strength; they shall mount up with wings like eagles; they shall run and not be weary; they shall walk and not faint." (Isaiah 40:31)
- "The Lord is good to those who wait for him, to the soul who seeks him. It is good that one should wait quietly for the salvation of the Lord." (Lamentations 3:25–26)

Chapter 3 ends on a note of high drama and suspense. Will the closer relative step in to redeem Ruth? Will Boaz and Ruth move toward marriage? Will Ruth and Naomi finally be redeemed? Our attention now turns in Chapter 4 to the character of Boaz, the "worthy man" who brings this story to a conclusion.

QUESTIONS FOR PERSONAL APPLICATION AND REFLECTION

1. Naomi and Ruth implemented a plan that required taking some risks. Think about a time in your life when God led you to step out in faith and make a courageous decision. How did the providence of God work that situation in your life? Are you facing any decisions in your life that require boldness and courage?

2. C.H. Spurgeon was asked how he reconciled the truths of divine sovereignty and human responsibility. He replied, "I never reconcile two friends." What happens when we lose the balance between prayer and human action? What steps do you need to take in order to fulfill your present responsibilities?

3. The church father Augustine defined virtue as a rightly ordered love. He said that we are prone to "love too much what should be loved less." What are the lesser loves in our lives that can take first place in our hearts? How can we make sure that our love for God is primary in our affections?

4. Boaz and Ruth didn't have much in common from an earthly perspective, yet their relationship was a match made in heaven. What practical lessons can we learn from their relationship? How can single believers in the church be encouraged to pursue healthy dating relationships?

5. Robert McQuilkin was faithful to his wife Muriel in sickness and in death. He understood that marriage is a covenant worth keeping. What are the keys to sustaining a faithful commitment in marriage over decades? What trends do you see in our society that challenge such a commitment?

CHAPTER 7

CONSIDER IT DONE

RUTH 4:1-12

Dr. Harry Ironside was a wonderful Bible teacher in the early decades of the 20th century. On one occasion while speaking on the campus of a Christian college, he was approached by a student after his sermon and was asked this question: "How do you manage to get up every morning and study the Bible?" I love Dr. Ironside's response. He said, "I just get up."[1]

One of the keys to living a life of significance and success is simply doing what we ought to do, whether we are in the mood or not. Half the battle in life is just showing up. The famous basketball player Jerry West once said, "You can't get much done if you only work on the days when you feel good."[2] We are called to rise to the challenges that life sets before us.

The Bible speaks to the value of hard work and persistence:

- "The hand of the diligent will rule, while the slothful will be put to forced labor." (Proverbs 12:24)
- "Whoever is slothful will not roast his game, but the diligent man will get precious wealth." (Proverbs 12:27)
- "The soul of the sluggard craves and gets nothing, while the soul of the diligent is richly supplied." (Proverbs 13:4)

Phyllis Moir served as Winston Churchill's secretary and described how diligent her boss was about his work. Before becoming prime minister, Churchill was anxious about the Nazi threat, but he also had a series of book deadlines. On the day Prague fell, he was hurrying to complete a 300,000-word history of the English people. He said after supper, "It's hard to take one's attentions off the events of today and concentrate on the reign of James II—but I'm going to do it." And he did. "When a job of writing has to be done," said Moir, "Mr. Churchill sits down to it whether he is in the mood or not and the effort generates his creative power."[3]

That's a great example for us all! With the thought of diligence in mind, let's re-enter the story of Ruth, Naomi and Boaz. The previous chapter ended in heart-pounding suspense. Boaz had promised to marry Ruth through levirate marriage (3:11–13, 4:9–10). There was a wrinkle, however, with the existence of a closer relative. This man lawfully had to be given the first opportunity to marry Ruth. As Chapter 3 ends, Naomi and Ruth are left waiting to see how the matter would turn out.

In this chapter, the character of Boaz comes into full view. It's his time to shine. While God is the ultimate hero of this story, Boaz is the immediate hero. He is a kind of savior for both Ruth and Naomi. As the human savior, he will ride to the rescue of these widows. He will follow through on his promise and get the job done!

THE MAN

Now Boaz had gone up to the gate and sat down there. And behold, the redeemer, of whom Boaz had spoken, came by. So Boaz said, "Turn aside, friend; sit down here." And he turned aside and sat down. And he took ten men of the elders of the city and said, "Sit down here." So they sat down. (Ruth 4:1–2)

Boaz is a model of manliness. He is a man of strength, substance and virtue. He is also a model of everyday discipleship. The events of this chapter do not take place in the tent of meeting or in the place of worship. Instead, they take place at the city gate, which is where commerce took place in that society. Boaz lives out his loyal love for God in the place where everyday business is conducted.

Boaz acted with immediacy

There is no discernible gap between the end of Chapter 3 and the beginning of Chapter 4. The sun that had risen would not be allowed to set until the matter was concluded. Boaz acted without delay. He was determined to get this thing done in a day. This is a guy who delivered on his promise!

James Fraser, the great missionary to the Lisu people of China, found that this was often his own greatest obstacle to fruitful ministry. He wrote in his diary:

> The temptation I have often had to contend with is persistent under many forms: "If only I were in such and such a position" for example, "shouldn't I be able to do a great work!… It is all IF and WHEN. I believe the devil is fond of those conjunctions … The plain truth is that the Scriptures never teach us to wait for opportunities of service, but to serve in just the things that lie next to our hands … The Lord bids us work, watch and pray; but Satan suggests, wait until a good opportunity for working, watching, and praying presents itself—and needless to say, this opportunity is always in the future.[4]

In this chapter, there is no "if and when" with Boaz! He immediately sets out to take care of business. When he arrives at the gate, he encounters the near relative who happened to be passing by at the same time. Again, we see the providence of God working in this story. Boaz was in the right place at the right time!

Arnold Palmer is one of the great golfers in history. He was brilliant on the course and beloved off the course. Over a span of 60 years he earned 62 PGA title wins. Arnie's army dubbed him "the King." He famously said, "The more I practice, the luckier I get."[5]

The truth is that divine providence blesses human effort. Understanding the providence of God will not make us passive. Instead it will make us bold and courageous. We know that God's providence will work with us and for us. With this understanding, we can pursue our goals with diligence!

Remember the Old Testament story of Joseph. His brothers sold him into slavery. Potiphar's wife tried to seduce him in Egypt. Joseph went to prison. Things looked dark and hopeless. Yet by the end of the story, Joseph was in charge of the domestic affairs of the kingdom of Egypt.

The life of Joseph is a wonderful testimony to the sovereignty of God (Genesis 50:20). Yet the story does not unfold apart from human initiative and diligence. When Joseph was in prison and in Potiphar's home, he didn't roll over and play dead. Genesis 39:3 says, "the Lord caused all that he did to succeed in his hands." Joseph trusted God and acted in difficult circumstances. He worked hard and God blessed his efforts.

Dear friend, do you have a responsibility to fulfill? Don't sleep until your duty is accomplished. Don't let procrastination hinder you from following through with your obligations. May God's kind providence bless your labors!

Boaz was marked by integrity

Boaz goes to the city gate, which was in the public square. This was the place where legal matters were recorded. There were 10 elders present, which means that there were public witnesses. The entire transaction was above board and properly executed.

Boaz was a man of influence in the city. He could have gone to city hall and gathered some of his friends. He could have carved out a favorable deal on the side. But he didn't do any of those things. Boaz wanted to marry Ruth, but he wanted to do things legally and ethically. He had to conduct his pursuit of Ruth in the proper manner.

Integrity is the idea that we are the same person in the dark that we are in the light. It means that we are governed by core values and not by expediency or situational ethics. The word "integrity" describes the idea of wholeness, soundness and integration. A person of integrity is marked by consistent character and commitment.

Professional golfer Tom Watson at an early age had his heart set on being a champion. He also had his personal code of honor firmly in mind. In the first state tournament that he ever endured, he put his putter down behind the ball on one of the greens. To his dismay, the ball moved slightly. No one saw it—of that he was certain. He was under great pressure to win, and there was no time to add up the pluses and minuses of the alternatives. But he knew without hesitation what he must do. He went over to an official and said, "My ball moved." That action cost him a stroke, and he lost the hole. Tom Watson placed his personal integrity ahead of his keen desire to win.[6]

To live with integrity will come at a cost. Yet the Bible speaks to the value of a life of integrity:

- "Vindicate me, O LORD, for I have walked in my integrity, and I have trusted in the LORD without wavering." (Psalm 26:1)
- "But you have upheld me because of my integrity, and set me in your presence forever." (Psalm 41:12)
- "For the LORD God is a sun and shield; the Lord bestows favor and honor. No good thing does he withhold from those who walk uprightly." (Psalm 84:11)

Integrity means that we are not playing a religious game. It means that we are not walking in hypocrisy. Plagiarism in the pastorate is a lack of integrity. Committing yourself to a church membership covenant and then failing to attend or serve is a lack of integrity. Sneaking away from work early is a lack of integrity, as is professing to love God while hating your neighbor. Condemning sexual sin while secretly watching pornography is a lack of integrity.

William Gladstone was an English political statesman who lived in the 19th century. His deep Christian faith shaped his politics. Gladstone served many years in the British parliament and four terms as a prime minister. The highly respected Baptist preacher, Charles Spurgeon, lived at the same time as Gladstone. Spurgeon once said of Gladstone, "We believe in no man's infallibility, but it is restful to feel sure of one man's integrity."[7]

Proverbs 22:1 says, "A good name is to be chosen rather than great riches, and favor is better than silver or gold." It is good to know those who walk with integrity. Boaz was that type of man. Ruth and Naomi found assurance in Boaz's trusted character, and they knew that he would follow through with his commitments.

Boaz was marked by intelligence

> *Then he said to the redeemer, "Naomi, who has come back from the country of Moab, is selling the parcel of land that belonged to our relative Elimelech. So I thought I would tell you of it and say, 'Buy it in the presence of those sitting here and in the presence of the elders of my people.' If you will redeem it, redeem it. But if you will not, tell me, that I may know, for there is no one besides you to redeem it, and I come after you." And he said, "I will redeem it." Then Boaz said, "The day you buy the field from the hand of Naomi, you also acquire Ruth the Moabite, the widow of the dead, in order to perpetuate the name of the dead in his inheritance." (Ruth 4:3–5)*

Boaz meets with the near relative at the city gate and proceeds to handle the dialogue with skill and wisdom. Boaz presents the opportunity in two parts: first, he talks about the land in relation to Naomi. Second, he mentions the obligation to marry the widow Ruth. The order is deliberate and well-timed. The dialogue is designed to give Boaz a fighting chance to have Ruth become his wife.

According to the concept of levirate marriage, the relative would be obligated to raise a son with Ruth. The sticking point is that when the son is old enough, he will take the land back on behalf of the household of Elimelech. The relative agrees to the first part of the deal but stumbles over the second. He wants to keep the land in his household in perpetuity. David Atkinson writes, "Here Boaz' deep personal care for Ruth shines through. It was in order that he might marry her that Boaz had engineered this ploy, mentioning the land first, and Ruth afterwards. And his 'masterstroke' came off."[8]

We note Boaz's negotiation skills in this passage. Because his goal was not to make money but to marry Ruth, he knew when to share knowledge and when to withhold it. He exercised restraint and self-control. He played his cards right and won Ruth as his wife!

Paul Miller observes that Boaz uses the following principles of good negotiation in this meeting:

1. Let the other party name the first price and make the first move
2. Be willing to walk
3. Know our opponent
4. Play your cards close
5. Know your goal[9]

Here is a man who knew how to conduct his business! Biblical wisdom is characterized not only by book smarts but also the ability to deal wisely in earthly affairs. The Proverbs extol the character trait of prudence:

- "O simple ones, learn prudence; O fools, learn sense." (Proverbs 8:5)
- "A prudent man conceals knowledge, but the heart of fools proclaims folly." (Proverbs 12:23)
- "The simple inherit folly, but the prudent are crowned with knowledge." (Proverbs 14:18)

Prudence is marked by cautious optimism, measured emotions, and the ability to implement well-laid plans. Boaz lived out this quality. Paul Miller writes, "Boaz is all man here. Solemn. Strong. Authoritative. Clear. Careful. The precision of his legal language—an example of prudence—removes any ambiguity that someone could exploit."[10] The wisdom of Boaz wins the day and sets up his eventual marriage to Ruth. He sets for us an example that is well worth following!

THE MEETING

Then the redeemer said, "I cannot redeem it for myself, lest I impair my own inheritance. Take my right of redemption yourself, for I cannot redeem it. Now this was the custom in former times in Israel concerning redeeming and exchanging: to confirm a transaction, the one drew off his sandal and gave it to the other, and this was the manner of attesting in Israel. So when the redeemer said to Boaz, "Buy it for yourself," he drew off his sandal. (Ruth 4:6–8)

The relative hands off to Boaz the responsibility of redeeming the land. This transfer is symbolized by the giving of a sandal to Boaz. The gesture was a kind of public notarization of the agreement. Once the sandal was given, the transaction was completed. Boaz could now move forward with marriage to Ruth.

What are we to make of the man who is the closer relative in this story? The text doesn't look too kindly upon this man. The term translated "friend" (4:1) in the Hebrew literally means "so-and-so." This anonymous man is viewed with a certain kind of disdain by the writer of this narrative. He rejected the opportunity to care for Naomi and marry Ruth.

Samuel Cox has stated:

> It is a curious comment on his narrow, selfish ambition that, of this man who was bent on preserving his name and fame, who would run no risk of having his name cut from his place, neither Israel nor the world even so much as remembers [his] mere name. His is unnamed in the very Book which recounts his story; we know him simply as the "anonymous kinsman"; while Boaz, who had no such selfish ambition, who held that in every nation they who trust God and work righteousness are acceptable with Him, lives on forever on the sacred page, and is enrolled, together with Ruth, in the pedigree of Him whose Name is above every name.[11]

Mr. So-and-So was more concerned about his inheritance than he was about the plight of two widows. He acts as a foil for the wonderful example of Boaz, the kinsman-redeemer. Boaz shines all the brighter in contrast to what this unnamed man failed to do. Boaz's name is spoken of to this day; the other man's name is forgotten in history.

True love is voluntarily deciding to seek the highest good of the other person, regardless of the cost. You can't love on the cheap! Loving your neighbor will cost you time and money. Loving your wife will cost you your life. Loving your brother will cost you your preferences. Yet true love is powerful and changes the course of history. C.S. Lewis observed,

> To love at all is to be vulnerable. Love anything and your heart will be wrung and possibly broken. If you want to make sure of keeping it intact you must give it to no one, not even an animal. Wrap it carefully round with hobbies and little luxuries; avoid all entanglements. Lock it up safe in the casket or coffin of your selfishness. But in that casket, safe, dark, motionless, airless, it will change. It will not be broken; it will become unbreakable, impenetrable, irredeemable. To love is to be vulnerable.[12]

Boaz understood and embraced the cost of true love. There is a famous painting by John Singer Sargent, who lived in the early 20th century. He was approached by Miss Elizabeth Garrett, the founder of Johns Hopkins Medical School, to paint a group portrait of the four men who had brought renown to that institution: Drs. Welch, Halstead, Osler and Kelly. From the very beginning, Dr. Welch did not get along with Sargent. He complained that Sargent called them all "Kelly" and objected to the way that they were posed. John Sargent got so angry that he told Welch that he would paint him so that his facial features would gradually fade and he would not be remembered by posterity. The painting of the "Four Doctors" still hangs in the Medical School of Johns Hopkins University, but the face of Dr. William Henry Welch is steadily fading. Those who walk the halls of this prestigious university can no longer discern what Dr. Welch looked like.[13]

There are those like Mr. So-and-So who only look out for themselves. Their names gradually fade away in history. There are others like Boaz who give themselves on behalf of others. These are the names which live on in history!

THE MARRIAGE

> Then Boaz said to the elders and all the people, "You are witnesses this day that I have bought from the hand of Naomi all that belonged to Elimelech and all that belonged to Chilion and to Mahlon. Also Ruth the Moabite, the widow of Mahlon, I have bought to be my wife, to perpetuate the name of the dead in his inheritance, that the name of

> *the dead may not be cut off from among his brothers and from the gate of his native place. You are witnesses this day." Then all the people who were at the gate and the elders said, "We are witnesses. May the LORD make the woman, who is coming into your house, like Rachel and Leah, who together built up the house of Israel. May you act worthily in Ephrathah and be renowned in Bethlehem, and may your house be like the house of Perez, whom Tamar bore to Judah, because of the offspring that the LORD will give you by this young woman." (Ruth 4:9–12)*

What a great moment in this story! Boaz announces his love for Ruth loudly before all the people in the community. His public pronouncement is an occasion for great joy and celebration.

The story is told of a man and woman who were making their wedding vows during their marriage ceremony. The minister asked the groom, "Will you take this woman to be your lawful wedded wife?" He replied, "Well, I've been thinking actually …" The minister responded, "Well, it is good that you have been thinking but actually I have asked you a question, 'Will you?'" The groom said, "Well, I get very excited when I think about her." The minister persisted, "I'm very glad you get excited when you think about her, but the question I am asking you is, 'Will you?'" The man said, "I will." The minister then turned to the bride and asked, "Will you take this idiot to be your lawful wedded husband?"[14]

You can be sure that Boaz had no such problem making a public commitment. He allows the community to share his joy in his intentions to marry Ruth. The scene ends with the prospect that Boaz and Ruth will be given offspring. I once heard a pastor pray for a young couple: "May God give you the patience of Job, the wisdom of Samuel and the children of Israel!" This thought is picked up in the prayers of the townsfolk:

- In verse 11, the people pray that God would make Ruth "like Rachel and Leah, who together built up the house of Israel." These were the founding mothers of the nation of Israel.
- "The house of Perez" referenced in verse 12 was one of the leading houses in the tribe of Judah, which was considered the

chief tribe in Israel. The people wish that Boaz and Ruth would establish a similarly important family in Judah.

I have often quoted the statement: "There is no success without succession."[15] When we die, we want our names to live on through marriage and children. Our lives can continue to be influential through the children we have raised. If God is gracious, the impact of a godly life will be seen in generations that are still to come.

Noel Piper writes about this type of influence in her biographical account of Sarah Edwards. Sarah was married to Jonathan, the great theologian and preacher. The Edwardses had 10 children and raised them faithfully. Generations later, a study was made contrasting two families. Noel Piper writes, "One had hundreds of descendants who were a drain on society. The other, descendants of Jonathan and Sarah Edwards, were outstanding for their contributions to society."[16] When over 1,400 descendants of the Edwards family were surveyed, it was found that this marriage had produced:

- Thirteen college presidents
- Sixty-five professors
- One hundred lawyers and a dean of a law school
- Thirty judges
- Sixty-six physicians and a dean of a medical school
- Eighty holders of public office[17]

Journalist A.E. Winship said this about the influence of Jonathan and Sarah over generations: "Members of the family wrote 135 books ... edited 18 journals and periodicals. They entered the ministry in platoons and sent one hundred missionaries overseas, as well as stocking many mission boards with lay trustees."[18] He concludes, "There is scarcely a Great American industry that has not had one of this family among its chief promoters."[19]

What a great encouragement to invest in the next generation! It is a blessing to see your children's children (Psalm 128:6). I want to bring my children up in the fear and admonition of the Lord. I pray that my children will honor me all the days of their lives. I also pray that their children will also honor them as well. And somehow, something will happen across the generations that is lasting and extends on into eternity. This is where I find my greatest joy. June and I are thrilled that, as I write this, we are about to see our children's children. There is a new generation emerging, and I pray that it will know and display God's grace and mercy.

St. Paul's Cathedral was destroyed in the Great Fire of 1666 in London. The present building was erected in 1675 by Christopher Wren and it was finished in 1708 by his son. Visitors are surprised that there is no memorial to Christopher Wren today in marble. His tomb is in the crypt near other massive tombs. On it, a plaque bears the Latin inscription, *"Si momumentum requiris, circumspice."* Translated into English it reads: "If you seek his monument, look around you."[20]

C.H. Spurgeon said, "A good character is the best tombstone. Those who loved you and were helped by you will remember you when forget-me-nots have withered. Carve your name on hearts, not on marble."[21] If you write your name on your children's hearts, they will be living monuments to your life and legacy. Boaz and Ruth were privileged to know this blessing. The child would go on to be the grandfather of David. From David's line would come the Messiah, the Lord Jesus Christ. The impact of Boaz and Ruth would be felt across many generations. It is still being experienced in the world today!

At the end of this scene, Boaz has skillfully negotiated the right to marry Ruth. He has publicly announced his intentions, and it is a celebratory moment filled with happiness and joy. Boaz will fulfill his role as the kinsman-redeemer. If the story were to end here, it would be a wonderful resolution to a story that has been filled with twists and turns. But God is always doing more than we can ask or think. The narrative continues on to an even more satisfying conclusion. Everybody loves a happy ending and Ruth certainly has one!

QUESTIONS FOR PERSONAL APPLICATION AND REFLECTION

1. Boaz expressed his loyal love for God in the place where everyday business was conducted. Where is the place in which God has called you to live out your faith? How can you honor Him more in your daily responsibilities?

2. Boaz immediately set out to deliver on the promise he made to Ruth and Naomi. Examine how procrastination shows up in our everyday lives. Why do you think Boaz moved so quickly in fulfilling his commitment? What blessings come into our lives when we overcome procrastination?

3. Think about the statement: "Integrity is the idea that we are the same person in the dark that we are in the light." Why is integrity so valuable in our day and age? Who are the examples of integrity that you have admired in your life?

4. Boaz handled his negotiations with practical skill. Biblical wisdom is characterized not only by book smarts but also the ability to deal wisely in earthly affairs. Ask God to grow you in practical wisdom. Seek one or two mentors who will guide you in developing this character quality in your life.

5. Boaz's name is still spoken of to this day. Mr. So-and-so has been forgotten in history. A life of faithful love leaves a legacy for others to follow. Who are the people in your life that God has called you to love? What are some practical ways that you can show your loyalty and faithfulness?

CHAPTER 8

EVERYBODY LOVES A HAPPY ENDING

RUTH 4:13-22

A growing number of movies today don't have a happy ending. The hero doesn't live. The boy doesn't marry the girl. The answer never comes. Oftentimes, I find myself turning to my wife June at the end of a film and saying, "I can't believe it ended that way." At the end of many stories, there is so much left unsettled and unsaid.

Not all will agree with my gripe. A few years back, journalist Finlo Rohrer asked the question: "Why the obsession with happy endings?"[1] He observed that there are no happy endings when it comes to the world's problems today. If art is supposed to imitate life, can we really expect stories to have happy endings? Isn't life more like a Greek tragedy than a Disney fairy tale?

While the article makes a point, I believe that the human soul is wired to anticipate happy endings. We want to believe that the arc of history bends toward justice. We need to hold out the prospect that dreams do indeed come true. We all want to believe there is a reason to hope. We want something to look forward to!

I like the story of the little girl who had learned the fairy tale, "Snow White and the Seven Dwarfs." She was telling the story to her mother. When she got to the part where the prince kissed Snow White and awakened her from her sleep, the little girl said, "Mother, do you know what happened then?" The mother, knowing how the story ended, said, "They lived happily ever after." The little girl said, "Oh no, they got married."[2]

Sometimes we have different ideas of what makes for a happy ending. But there is no question that the book of Ruth provides one. The narrative moves from personal tragedy to joyful triumph. The story ends with a wedding celebration and the birth of a baby boy. And then, God further exceeds our expectations by weaving this narrative into the greater story of the building of His kingdom. From this humble account of ordinary individuals in a little town called Bethlehem comes the epic story of the coming of Messiah—the king of Israel who will bring salvation to the nations. The final verses of the book give us much more than we bargained for.

The story is told of a visiting pastor who was attending a men's breakfast in a rural area. He asked one of the older farmers in attendance to say grace that morning. After all were seated, the older farmer began, "Lord, I hate buttermilk."

The pastor opened one eye and wondered to himself where this was going.

The farmer then loudly proclaimed, "Lord, I hate lard."

Now the pastor was worried.

However, without missing a beat, the farmer prayed on. "And Lord, you know I don't care much for raw white flour."

Just as the pastor was ready to stand and stop everything, the farmer continued, "But Lord, when you mix 'em all together and bake 'em up, I do love fresh biscuits. So Lord, when things come up we don't like, when life gets hard, when we just don't understand what you are sayin' to us, we need to relax and wait 'till You are done mixin', and probably it will be somethin' even better than biscuits ... Amen."[3]

It was an unorthodox prayer, but the prayer was full of orthodoxy! When God is done mixing all the elements of our lives together, they end up working together for our good (Romans 8:28). What is broken, He mends. What is crooked, He makes straight. What is bad, he turns to good. The book of Ruth is about a family who fell apart; God put them back together. This truth speaks comfort into each of our lives. All of history is moving toward a happy ending!

GOD'S GIFT

So Boaz took Ruth, and she became his wife. And he went in to her, and the LORD gave her conception, and she bore a son. (Ruth 4:13)

Without wasting any time, the narrator leapfrogs over the wedding celebrations to focus on the birth of a baby boy. We read of Boaz "taking" Ruth from the home of Naomi and bringing her to his home. The language emphasizes not only a change in location but a change in status. Ruth is no longer the foreign Moabite; she is now the wife of Boaz. She has been fully accepted into the covenant community of Israel.

This is obviously a heterosexual marriage between a man and a woman. The union is publicly witnessed and celebrated by friends and family. The marriage is then consummated in the bedroom chamber. The sexual union takes place within the context of a covenant relationship. It leads to pregnancy and the birth of a baby boy. Marriage and children are gifts from the Lord. Let us consider how precious these blessings are.

The provision

The Lord is directly mentioned in the book of Ruth only two times (1:6, 4:13). These two references highlight the blessings of food and fertility. God grants the gift of life as well as the means to sustain that life. David Strain comments, "The LORD is visiting His people again, not to give them food this time, but to give them a child. It's a beautiful way to underscore that this baby is not like any other born in Israel in those days. This baby was a child of promise, a child of destiny. His arrival was the result of a divine visitation."[4]

The Bible emphasizes that children are a gift of God. Naomi and Ruth have done everything in their power to improve their situation. They have labored and planned and acted with boldness. But at the end of the day, it is the Lord who blesses their home. In the end, this is not a story about self-made women. It is a story of God's blessing and divine favor!

I recently watched a movie with June and our three daughters. It was the latest version of the movie, *Little Women*.[5] (Guys, just to defend my manhood, I will say that real men watch the movie *Little Women*.) At the end of the film, my daughter Angela pointed out a particular scene where the fictional character named Beth is given a piano from a wealthy benefactor. The sisters are excited about the piano and describe to Beth all the things that she will do with it. In the middle of all the hullabaloo, Beth leaves unnoticed and heads next door to say thank you. Angela pointed out that while the sisters focused on the gift, Beth made sure she thanked the giver!

So often in life, we are like those sisters who stand over the gifts of God and neglect to thank the giver. The blessings that enrich our lives are postmarked from heaven. Let us learn to slip away, go into God's presence and give thanks. Let us show gratitude to God, the giver of all good things!

The pattern

Genesis 2:24 says, "Therefore a man shall leave his father and his mother and hold fast to his wife, and they shall become one flesh." The marriage of Boaz and Ruth followed the biblical pattern. Marriage is a creation ordinance and we don't have the right to redefine it. God's design for marriage is given for our blessing. We must preserve and protect the institution of marriage.

History shows us that the disintegration of the heterosexual family spells the end of a country's health and wealth. Recently the Joint Economic Committee of Congress produced a study entitled, "The Demise of the Happy Two-Parent Home." This report describes the collapse of marriage and the traditional family in America:

- In 1962, 71 percent of women ages 15–44 were married. By 2019, this was down to 42 percent.
- In 1962, 5 percent of women ages 30–34 had never been married. By 2019, this was up to 35 percent.
- In the 1960s, less than 1 percent of couples living together were not married. Today, it is over 12 percent.

- In 1970, 85 percent of children lived with two parents. By 2019, this was down to 70 percent.[6]

The breakdown of the family unit is catastrophic to a nation. God's plan is for children to be raised by two parents who are bound together in the covenant of marriage. When you tinker with that formula, you undermine the health of society. Our country is seeing the devastating effects of such a failure.

The text speaks appropriately of the sexual relations between Boaz and Ruth: "And he went in to her, and the Lord gave her conception" (4:13). The married couple consummated their relationship in sexual union and a pregnancy resulted. David Atkinson writes, "The richness of the God-given significance to physical sexual relationship requires a context of permanent and committed love and faithfulness between the partners."[7] This narrative is a reminder that God's plan for sex within marriage is an expression of His grace and blessing.

The great preacher Adrian Rogers once remarked, "Fire in its place is a wonderful thing. It spreads light and dispels darkness, sets a welcoming mood, generates heat, invites conversation. In the hearth it is good but out of the hearth it will burn your house down."[8] Premarital and extramarital sex are sinful and God will judge them. Sex within marriage brings the greatest joy. The marriage of Boaz and Ruth is an example of faithful marital love!

The famous economist E.F. Schumacher once gave a talk where he recounted his visit to St. Petersburg, Russia. At the time, the city was under the rule of communism. Despite having a map in his hand, he realized he was lost. What he saw on paper didn't fit what was in front of his eyes. Around him, he saw several huge Russian Orthodox churches. They weren't on the map and yet he was certain he knew what street he was on. "Ah," said the Soviet tourist guide, trying to be helpful. "That's simple. We don't show churches on our maps."

Schumacher went on to say this: "It then occurred to me that this is not the first time I had been given a map which failed to show things I could see right in front of my life."[9] That's a great insight! If you follow the world's roadmap for life and marriage you will inevitably find yourself to be lost. The secular media's depiction of love, sex and romance leaves out the most important realities of life. God created marriage to be a covenant relationship that is permanent until death. In this union, true love is expressed in a commitment that endures through the trials and the difficulties of life. Ruth and Boaz entered into this relationship and received the blessing of marriage. Let us learn to uphold the biblical pattern of marriage so that God may be glorified in our lives!

The principle

The text says that God gave Ruth conception (4:13). That verse teaches a very important principle: *the gift of life was the blessing of God.* The Bible teaches that human life begins at conception. Let us consider the importance of this truth in relation to the times in which we live.

David said in Psalm 139:15, "My frame was not hidden from you, when I was being made in secret, intricately woven in the depths of the earth." J. Carl Laney writes, "Not only is God active in the event of conception itself, but He is personally involved in the formation and development of the human baby in the mother's womb."[10] A child being formed in the mother's womb is not the result of random chance or natural selection. God is the giver and sustainer of life!

Exodus 21:22 depicts a scenario in which a pregnant woman was struck. If harm resulted to the child in her womb, the penalty would be "life for life, eye for eye, tooth for tooth, hand for hand, foot for foot, burn for burn, wound for sound, stripe for stripe" (Exodus 21:23–24). The life of an unborn child was protected by the law of Moses. Ronald Allen concludes, "The Bible never speaks of fetal life as mere chemical activity, cellular growth or vague force. Rather, the fetus in the mother's womb is … being shaped, fashioned, molded and woven together by the personal activity of God."[11]

A British newspaper carried the story of a London motorist who received a parking fine. This man woke up flummoxed by the fact that his car was parked in a disabled bay. There was a fine on his windshield for the equivalent of $158 USD. During the night, the city of London had decided to restripe the streets. The man had parked legally the night before, but the city council had decided that a certain portion of the road would become reserved parking. A change had happened without him noticing and he ended up having to pay a price.[12]

Many Christians can identify with the feeling of this motorist. We increasingly feel that we are waking up to a culture in which the laws are being rewritten. Al Mohler writes:

> The pro-abortion movement has sown a culture of death. It attempts to destroy and to deny the sanctity of life, and the consequences are now clear to see. This is what happens when a society jettisons the moral code based in the truth that every human is an extension of God's common grace, and a bearer of God's image. Unless this march to death is reversed, the headlines will only become more horrifying and even deadlier.[13]

In these dark times, Christians are called to shine God's light. The church is called to be what the society is not. The Bible calls us to defend the rights of those who cannot defend themselves: "Open your mouth, judge righteously, defend the rights of the poor and needy" (Proverbs 31:9). There are many ways that we can be involved in promoting a culture of life. Believers can support and volunteer at local pregnancy centers. A number of the families in my church are involved in foster care and some have been led to adopt children. Perhaps God will give some young men and women a passion to fight for just laws in our society. May the church come alongside women who are struggling and give emotional, physical and spiritual support. May we be involved in the protection and the preservation of life!

GOD'S GOODNESS

Then the women said to Naomi, "Blessed be the LORD, who has not left you this day without a redeemer, and may his name be renowned in Israel! He shall be to you a restorer of life and a nourisher of your old age, for your daughter-in-law who loves you, who is more to you than seven sons, has given birth to him." Then Naomi took the child and laid him on her lap and became his nurse. And the women of the neigh-

> *borhood gave him a name, saying, "A son has been born to Naomi."*
> *They named him Obed. He was the father of Jesse, the father of David.*
> *(Ruth 4:14–17)*

Let's get back to the wonderful narrative of Ruth. In this final scene, we see the story come full circle. You will observe that the narrative here shines a spotlight on Naomi, as Ruth and Boaz fade into the background. Naomi's bitter experience has turned into blessing. She came back to Bethlehem empty, but now she is full. She had doubted God's goodness but He has shown Himself faithful.

This is a beautiful scene of joyful celebration. The women in the community recognize the fact that God has blessed Naomi abundantly. God has given Ruth conception and granted Naomi a grandson. The child will take care of Naomi in old age. In addition, Naomi's daughter-in-law Ruth is worth more than the value of seven sons.

God is clearly preoccupied with Naomi's welfare and well-being. We noted earlier that the book of Ruth returns to focus on Naomi at the end of every chapter. The literary repetition in the book is theologically weighty. God has shown His faithful care in Naomi's life.

This story reminds us of God's faithful care for His people. Friend, perhaps you need to hear this truth today. First Peter 5:7 says that you can cast "all your anxieties on him, because he cares for you." I love the imagery of Deuteronomy 32:10 which says that God kept Israel "as the apple of His eye." Erik Raymond comments, "When you look into someone's eye, you can see yourself reflected in the pupil of their eyeball as a little person. Also, your eye is the most vulnerable part of your body. You protect it by blinking or turning your face … When we think about this term we should think of presence and protection."[14]

Our faithful God never leaves or forsakes His people. Like Naomi, we may find ourselves doubting God's goodness in the midst of heartbreaking circumstances. But if we live long enough, we will look back and recount God's provision for all of our needs. We will know that He has been with us in every season of life.

GOD'S GOVERNMENT

Now these are the generations of Perez: Perez fathered Hezron, Hezron fathered Ram, Ram fathered Amminadab, Amminadab fathered Nahshon, Nahshon fathered Salmon, Salmon fathered Boaz, Boaz fathered Obed, Obed fathered Jesse, and Jesse fathered David. (Ruth 4:18–22)

The book finishes with a wide-angle-lens perspective. The events in this narrative are folded into the grand redemptive story. The closing genealogy helps us to see that God did more than rescue two widows from poverty. The child born to Ruth and Boaz will be part of a line that will bring about the house of David the king. In 2 Samuel 7, God will make a covenant with David to "establish the throne of his kingdom forever" (verse 13). This is not merely a story about three individuals—it is an episode in the unfolding of God's kingdom!

Remember that in the beginning of Ruth, we read that the name Elimelech means "God is king." Yet the period of the judges was marked by rebellion and moral apostasy. From a human perspective, there was no king in Israel. The book of Ruth brings us to focus on the little town of Bethlehem, where a faithful man named Boaz lived out his everyday faith in the public square. Through ordinary acts of kindness, he redeemed Naomi and Ruth and provided for those two women. Through his actions, God graciously included them in the line of David. From the line of David will come another king—the Lord Jesus Christ. In this narrative, God shows that He was indeed king over Israel. The entire time, God was doing a work to establish His ultimate rule.

The inclusion of Ruth into the genealogy of the Messiah is a testimony of God's love for the nations. Daniel Block, in his excellent commentary on Ruth, notes that this is an inversion of the pattern we might expect. The Biblical writers were often fascinated with showing the rise of an Israelite in a foreign land—Joseph in Egypt, Daniel in Babylon. But in this story, we see the reverse of the normal pattern.[15]

Here we see the rise of a Moabite woman within Israel! Ruth is incorporated into the line of King David and of King Jesus. In Matthew 1, we find Tamar, Rahab, and Bathsheba in the genealogy of Jesus.

Tamar seduced her father-in-law to get pregnant, Rahab was a prostitute, Bathsheba committed adultery, and Ruth was a Moabite. And yet they are incorporated into the family line of the King of kings and Lord of lords! Their inclusion shows the gracious heart of God towards sinners. Boaz redeemed Ruth and Naomi from physical destitution. Jesus Christ redeems us from eternal destruction!

The story is told of a father who wanted to read a magazine but was being bothered by his little girl, Shelby. She wanted to know what the United States looked like. Finally, he tore out of his new magazine the page on which the United States map was printed. Tearing it into small pieces, he gave it to Shelby and said, "Go into the other room and see if you can put this together. This will show you our whole country today." After a few minutes, Shelby returned and handed him the map, correctly fitted and taped together. The father was surprised and asked how she had finished so quickly. "Oh," she said, "on the other side of the paper is a picture of Jesus. When I got Jesus back where He belonged, then our country just came together."[16]

I love that story! It is true for the book of Ruth as well: when the pieces of the story are put together, you will find there is a clear portrait of Jesus Christ. From Boaz comes Obed, from Obed comes David, and from David comes Jesus—the Savior of the world. Jesus Christ was fully God and fully man. He lived a perfect life in obedience to God's law. He died at the cross as a substitute for our sins. On the third day, He rose again from the grave! He offers forgiveness of sins and eternal life for any who will believe in His name. The apostles proclaimed, "There is salvation in no one else, for there is no other name under heaven given among men by which we must be saved" (Acts 4:12).

Friend, I don't care who you are or where you're from. I don't care what you have done in your past. There is no one beyond the reach of God's grace. In the book of Ruth, we see God's heart for sinners like you and me. John 3:16 says: "For God so loved the world, that he gave his only Son, that whoever believes in him should not perish but have eternal life." Jesus didn't come to condemn the world but to save it. He gave His life to bring salvation to the world!

I remember the story of the children in a prominent family who decided to give their father a book of the family's history. They commissioned a professional biographer to do the work, carefully warning him of the family's "black sheep" problem: Uncle George had been executed in the electric chair for murder. The biographer assured the children, "I can handle that situation so that there will be no embarrassment. I'll merely say that Uncle George occupied a chair of applied electronics at an important government institution. He was attached to his position by the strongest of ties and his death came as a real shock."[17]

Talk about whitewashing the black sheep! The Bible tells us that Jesus washes many black sheep. The outsider can become the insider. The lawless can indeed be justified. The destitute can be redeemed. The hopeless can be brought into a story of eternal hope. Grace included sinners in the family tree of the Messiah because, on another tree, Jesus demonstrated the redeeming love of God. At Calvary, Jesus Christ died in our place for our sins, so that we may be forgiven of all our sins and have eternal life.

Who doesn't love a happy ending? The story of Ruth, Boaz and Naomi certainly has one. But their story points to the happiest ending of all. Those who trust in Jesus Christ for salvation will live forever in His presence. His eternal kingdom will endure forever. His people will live happily ever after. "They will need no light of lamp or sun, for the Lord God will be their light, and they will reign forever and ever" (Revelation 22:5). May your heart know the beauty of His grace this day. May God strengthen your *everyday faith,* to His glory!

QUESTIONS FOR PERSONAL APPLICATION AND REFLECTION

1. "The human soul is wired to anticipate happy endings." Would you agree with this statement? Why or why not? How does the book of Ruth provide an ending that is even beyond our expectations?

2. Sometimes we can be so focused on the blessings of life that we forget to thank God who is the giver of all good things. What are some specific blessings that you are thankful for today? Take time in prayer to thank God for all of His benefits.

3. The book of Ruth celebrates the conception of a child in the mother's womb. We live in a society in which the sanctity of life is under assault. How can we as Christians shine God's light in the darkness? Are there any practical ways that we can be involved in the preservation and protection of unborn lives?

4. Compare Ruth 1:19–22 with Ruth 4:13–17. How has God shown His faithful care in Naomi's life? How does this story encourage you when you are tempted to doubt God's goodness and faithfulness?

5. The genealogy of Jesus is not a roll call of Israel's best but a lineage stained and sullied by black sheep. What does the genealogy of Jesus teach us about the magnitude of God's grace? How can we apply this understanding to our lives and our ministries?

CONCLUSION

There is nothing spectacular in the narrative of the book of Ruth. There are no dazzling displays of God's power and might—no burning bushes, no parted seas. Instead, there is a hiddenness to God's presence in this story. The book is about love and loss and marriage and business and food—the mundane affairs of life! Yet through the lives of these people, God accomplished a magnificent work to build His kingdom and bring salvation to the world.

I was once at a political event where a speaker made a memorable statement. He said: "America loves its superheroes. But the real heroes are the everyday Americans who get up, love God, love their neighbors and love their country."[1] That statement resonated with me because so much of life is quite ordinary. We work and we play. We attend church and raise a family. Most days, our lives appear to be quite unremarkable. We seek to be faithful in the everyday affairs of life.

It is easy to get caught up in the exploits of prominent Christians—the "spiritual giants" of this world whose faith appears to move mountains. Yet the book of Ruth testifies to the power of ordinary people living out their faith in our churches and our communities. These are the real heroes in our midst! God does His work through immigrants and businessmen, husbands and wives, widows and mothers-in-law, grandparents and townsfolk—all living out their faith in the public square. He accomplishes his purposes not only through princes and mighty warriors, but also through people like Ruth, Naomi and Boaz. God does His work through people like you and me. God can use our lives to accomplish great things for His glory!

Romans 15:4 says, "For whatever was written in former days was written for our instruction, that through the endurance and through the encouragement of the Scriptures we might have hope." Friend, I pray that you will be encouraged to be faithful to serve the Lord wherever He has placed you. May the Lord who displayed such kindness to Ruth and Naomi show you favor as you seek to honor Him with your *everyday faith*. God is able to take our lives of quiet faithfulness and weave them into a greater story that is beyond all that we could ask or imagine.

ACKNOWLEDGMENTS

I want to express my gratitude to a number of people for making this project possible.

To the leaders and members of Kindred Community Church—thank you for your love, commitment and faithful support. It is a privilege to serve with you for the glory of Christ.

I am grateful to the staff and dedicated volunteers at our national radio ministry, Know The Truth. To Dean Samsvick, Jerry Motto, Danielle Bracey, Estella Roach and Phil Seifert—thank you for making my ministry a joy.

I want to especially thank Dan Nah for his friendship and assistance in bringing this project to completion. A special word of thanks goes to Joan Shim for her excellent editing through the writing of this manuscript.

I continue to be indebted to my wife, June, whose selfless love inspires me on a daily basis. To my three daughters, Laura, Angela and Beth—I am grateful for your loving support.

To my son-in-law, Nathan, and to my granddaughter, Lily—thank you for being God's blessing in my life.

May God receive all glory for the great things that He has done. He is worthy of all our devotion and praise!

Philip De Courcy
Anaheim Hills, California

ENDNOTES

INTRODUCTION
1. Charles M. Schultz, *The Complete Peanuts, Vol. 5: 1959–1960*.

CHAPTER 1: THE ORIGINAL CINDERELLA
1. Warren Wiersbe, *Put Your Life Back Together* (Wheaton, IL: Victor Books, 1985), 9–12.
2. David Hamilton's testimony is recounted in Melvin Tinker, *Veiled in Flesh: The Incarnation – What It Means and Why It Matters* (London: IVP, 2019), 15–16.
3. United States, Department of Defense. "News briefing by Secretary of Defense Donald Rumsfeld." 12 Feb. 2002. As quoted in Hart Seely; "The Poetry of D.H. Rumsfeld;" Slate; 2 April 2003; https://slate.com/news-and-politics/2003/04/the-poetry-of-donald-rumsfeld.html; accessed January 15, 2021.
4. Elisabeth Elliot, *Suffering Is Never for Nothing* (Nashville: B&H Publishing, 1982), 47.

CHAPTER 2: A COSTLY MOVE
1. Moody Bible Institute, *Today in the Word*, November 1989, 23.
2. United Kingdom, House of Commons. Speech by British Prime Minister Winston Churchill, to the House of Commons. 4 June 1940.
3. Alistair Begg with Elizabeth McQuoid, *Ruth: 30-Day Devotional* (London, Intervarsity Press, 2017), iv.
4. Tim Chester and Steve Timmis, *Total Church* (Wheaton: Crossway, 2008), 63.
5. Michael Kelley, *Boring: Finding an Extraordinary God in an Ordinary Life* (Nashville: B&H Publishing Group, 2013) 205–206.
6. Randy Alcorn, "Cumulative Daily Decisions, Courage in a Cause, and a Life of Endurance" in *Stand: A Call for the Endurance of the Saints*, editors John Piper and Justin Taylor (Wheaton: Crossway Books, 2008), 94.
7. Charles Haddon Spurgeon, "A Divine Challenge!" from *New Park Street Pulpit* Volume 6. April 22, 1860.
8. Anne Graham Lotz, *Heaven: My Father's House* (Nashville, TN: W Publishing Group, 2001), 37–38.

CHAPTER 3: THE ROAD BACK

1. A. Boyd Luter and Barry C. Davis, *Ruth and Esther: God Beyond the Seen* (Grand Rapids: Baker Book House, 1995), 29.
2. Ascribed to Lao Tzu. http://www.bbc.co.uk/worldservice/learningenglish/movingwords/shortlist/laotzu.shtml Accessed February 9, 2021.
3. Oswald Chambers, *My Utmost for His Highest,* updated edition (Grand Rapids: Discovery House, 1992), 470.
4. Phebe's testimony is recorded in Jonathan Edwards, *A Faithful Narrative of the Surprising Work of God* (Lawton, OK: Trumpet Press, 2019), 57–61. The story of Justin Edwards' conversion is recounted in John Currid, *Ruth: From Bitter to Sweet* in Welwyn Commentary Series (Wyoming, MI: Evangelical Press, 2012), 35–36.
5. Paul Miller, *A Loving Life: In a World of Broken Relationships* (Wheaton: Crossway, 2014), 48.
6. John Tucker, "The Woman Who Changed the World." Sermon, Milford Baptist Church, North Shore Auckland, New Zealand, September 19, 2004. http://www.bible.net.nz/TUCKER/sermon_20040919.htm. Accessed February 9, 2021.
7. Shane Idleman, "Don't Reject the Voice of God." Sermon, Westside Christian Fellowship, Leona Valley, CA. February 5, 2017. https://westsidechristianfellowship.org/audio/2517-dont-reject-the-voice-of-god-pastor-shane-idleman/
8. Barry G. Webb, *Judges and Ruth: God in Chaos,* Preaching the Word, ed. R. Kent Hughes (Wheaton: Crossway, 2015), 250–251.
9. "Life Tested," Preaching.com: Leading the Church. Proclaiming the Word, https://www.preaching.com/sermon-illustrations/life-tested/. Accessed February 9, 2021.
10. John Calvin, Preface to Commentary on the Psalms. https://www.ccel.org/ccel/calvin/calcom08.vi.html, Accessed February 9, 2021.
11. Dale Ralph Davis, "Nursery and History." Sermon, First Presbyterian Church, Columbia, South Carolina, August 31, 2014. https://www.sermonaudio.com/sermoninfo.asp?SID=93141314462. Accessed February 9, 2021.
12. Thomas Watson, *All Things For Good: An Exposition of Romans 8:28* (Shawnee, KS: Gideon House Books, 2015), 25–26.

13. John Flavel, *The Mystery of Providence* (1824; repr., Warrendale, PA: Ichthus Publications, 2014), 23.
14. Adapted from Kent Crockett, *Slaying Your Giants: Biblical Solutions to Everyday Problems* (Peabody, MA: Hendrickson Publishers, 2013), 8–9.
15. Michael Hodgin, *1001 Humorous Illustrations: Fresh, Timely and Compelling Illustrations for Public Speaking* (Grand Rapids: Zondervan, 2010), 668.
16. "Two Words," Ministry 127: Encouraging, Equipping and Engaging Ideas from Local Church Leaders, https://ministry127.com/resources/illustration/two-words. Accessed February 9, 2021.

CHAPTER 4: NOTHING JUST HAPPENS

1. James C. Humes, *Churchill: Speaker of the Century* (New York: Stein and Day, 1980), 6–9.
2. J. Vernon McGee, *Ezra, Nehemiah, and Esther* in Thru the Bible Commentary Series (Nashville: Thomas Nelson, 1991), 173.
3. John Calvin, *Institutes of the Christian Religion* (Grand Rapids: Eerdmans, 1981), Book I, 179.
4. Bertrand Russell, *Why I Am Not a Christian* (New York: Simon and Schuster, 1957), 107.
5. John Currid, *Ruth: From Bitter to Sweet* in Welwyn Commentary Series (Grand Rapids, MI: EP Books, 2012), 64.
6. David Atkinson, *The Message of Ruth* in The Bible Speaks Today Series, ed. J.A. Motyer (Downers Grove, IL: IVP Academic, 1974), 68.
7. "God's Perfect Leading." Accessed March 23, 2021. https://bible.org/series/249?page=617
8. Proverbs, The List of. "Latin Proverb: 'Providence assists not the idle.'" The List of World Proverbs, February 11, 2021. http://www.listofproverbs.com/source/l/latin_proverb/70104.htm.
9. "Concurrence," Merriam-Webster (Merriam-Webster), accessed February 12, 2021, https://www.merriam-webster.com/dictionary/concurrence.
10. Louis Berkhof, *Manual of Christian Doctrine* (Grand Rapids: Wm. B. Eerdmans Publishing Company, 1933, repr. 2002), 114.
11. John C. Maxwell, *Talent Is Never Enough: Discover the Choices That Will Take You Beyond Your Talent* (Nashville: Thomas Nelson, 2007), 54.

12. "Trust in God and Keep Your Powder Dry." Wikipedia. Wikimedia Foundation, January 27, 2021. https://en.wikipedia.org/wiki/Trust_in_God_and_keep_your_powder_dry.
13. John W. Reed, "Ruth" in the Bible Knowledge Commentary: Old Testament eds. John F. Walvoord and Roy B. Zuck (Colorado Springs: David C. Cook, 1985), 422.
14. Thomas Watson: Body of Divinity - Christian Classics Ethereal Library. Accessed February 12, 2021. https://www.ccel.org/ccel/watson/divinity.vi.xiv.html.
15. Henry Law, *The Gospel in Exodus* (North Charleston, SC: Jazzybee Verlag, 1867 repr. 2017). unknown.
16. Sinclair Ferguson, *Faithful God: An Exposition of the Book of Ruth* (Bryntirion, Wales: Bryntirion, 2005), 56–57.
17. Ferguson, *Faithful God*, 56–57.
18. Louis Berkhof: Summary of Christian Doctrine - Christian Classics Ethereal Library. Accessed February 12, 2021. https://ccel.org/ccel/berkhof/summary/summary.iii.vi.html.
19. Edward Bouverie Pusey, *Sermons During the Seasons from Advent to Whitsuntide*. 2nd ed. In Parochial Sermons Vol. II (Oxford: John Henry Parker, 1848), 93.
20. Jonathan Edwards, *A History of the Work of Redemption* (New York: Leavitt, Trow & Company, 1845) 511.
21. C.H. Spurgeon, *An All-Round Ministry: Addresses to Ministers and Students* (London: The Banner of Truth Trust, 1960), 4–6.

CHAPTER 5: FINDING FAVOR

1. Charles Haddon Spurgeon, *Feathers for Arrows* (New York: Sheldon & Company, 1870), 83.
2. Warren Wiersbe, "How to be Blessable," "Sermonindex.net Audio Sermons - Sermon Index," accessed February 16, 2021, https://www.sermonindex.net/modules/mydownloads/singlefile.php?lid=13531&commentView=itemComments.
3. A Boyd Luter and Barry C. Davis, *God Behind the Seen: Expositions of the Books of Ruth and Esther* (Grand Rapids: Baker Books, 1995), 51.
4. Elisabeth Elliot, *Suffering Is Never for Nothing* (Nashville: B&H Publishing Group, 2019), 41–43.

5. John Wooden with Steve Jamison, *Wooden: A Lifetime of Observations and Reflections On and Off the Court* (New York: McGraw Hill, 1997), 79.
6. L.B. Cowman, *Streams in the Desert,* vol. 2 (Uhrichsville, OH: 1928), 197.
7. Tony Evans, *Called for a Purpose: Daily Devotions to Help You Pursue God's Plan* (Eugene, OR: Harvest House Publishers, 2018), 109.
8. F.B. Meyer's story is recounted in Warren W. Wiersbe, *Listening to the Giants: A Guide to Good Reading and Preaching* (Grand Rapids: Baker Publishing Group, 1979), 92.
9. Paul W. Powell, *No Looking Back* (Self-Published, 2007), 64–65.
10. Daniel I. Block, *Ruth: The King Is Coming* in Zondervan Exegetical Commentary on the Old Testament (Grand Rapids: Zondervan, 2015), 155.
11. James Merritt, *In a World of Friends, Foes & Fools: Fathers Can Teach Their Kids to Know the Difference* (Self-Published with Xulon Press, 2008), 121.
12. "Reputation And Character." Sermon Central, December 12, 2010. https://www.sermoncentral.com/sermon-illustrations/77844/reputation-and-character-by-rodelio-mallari.
13. "If I Take Care of My Character, My Reputation Will Take Care of Itself." D. L. Moody: If I take care of my character, my reputation will take care of itself. Accessed February 16, 2021. https://www.quotes.net/quote/41941.
14. Joel C. Gregory, *Growing Pains for the Soul* (Waco, TX: Word Books, 1987), 60.
15. Story is recounted in William Revell Moody, *The Life of D.L. Moody, the Official Authorized Edition* (New York: Fleming H. Revell Company, 1900), 373–381.
16. Paul Miller, *A Loving Life: In a World of Broken Relationships* (Wheaton, IL: Crossway, 2014), 127.
17. Dale Ralph Davis, "Nursery and History." Sermon, First Presbyterian Church, Columbia, South Carolina, August 31, 2014. https://www.sermonaudio.com/sermoninfo.asp?SID=93141314462. Accessed February 9, 2021.
18. Golda Meir's 1948 fundraising tour is recounted in Francine Klagsbrun, *Lioness: Golda Meir and The Nation of Israel* (New York: Schocken Books, 2017), 349–352.
19. Gary Inrig, *Quality Friendship* (Chicago, Moody Publishers, 1988), 105.
20. Quoted from Roy Zuck, *The Speaker's Quotebook: Over 4,500 Illustrations and Quotations For All Occasions* (Grand Rapids: Kregel Publications, 1997), 327.

CHAPTER 6: COLD FEET

1. Tony Evans, *Being Single and Satisfied* (Chicago: Moody Publishers, 2002), 5.
2. Quote attributed to Mary Kay Ash, *Miracles Happen* (New York: HarperCollins, 2003), 1.
3. Robert L. Hubbard, Jr., *The Book of Ruth*. The New International Commentary on the Old Testament (Grand Rapids: William B. Eerdmans Publishing Company, 1988), 195.
4. Paul Miller, *A Loving Life* (Wheaton, IL: Crossway, 2014), 149.
5. *The Iron Lady,* directed by Phyllida Lloyd (20th Century Fox, 2011).
6. Robert L. Hubbard, *The Book of Ruth,* 204.
7. Attributed to William Faulker, "Three Famous Short Novels by William Faulkner," PenguinRandomhouse.com, accessed March 16, 2021, https://www.penguinrandomhouse.com/books/48434/three-famous-short-novels-by-william-faulkner/.
8. C.H. Spurgeon, "Jacob and Esau." Sermon, New Park Street Chapel, Southwark, January 16, 1859. https://www.ccel.org/ccel/spurgeon/sermons05.xvi.html.
9. Tony Reinke, *Newton on the Christian Life: To Live is Christ* (Wheaton, IL: Crossway, 2015), 21.
10. James E. Rosscup, Unpublished note.
11. Attributed to David L. Cooper. Andrew Meisler, "Biblical Research Studies Group," Biblical Research Studies Group, accessed March 16, 2021, http://www.biblicalresearch.info/.
12. Saint Augustine, *On Christian Teaching,* trans. R.P.H. Green (Oxford: Oxford University Press, 1997), 21.
13. C.S. Lewis, *Letters of C.S. Lewis* eds. W.H. Lewis and Walter Hooper (San Francisco, CA: HarperOne, 2017), 550.
14. Ruth 3:11, New American Standard Version.
15. Stephen Davey, *Ruth* (Apex, NC: Charity House Publishers, 2013), 78.
16. Robertson McQuilkin, "Living by Vows," *Christianity Today,* February 1, 2004. http://cgsdlifeinspirit.weebly.com/uploads/7/4/1/7/7417809/three_ct_articles_together.pdf
17. Alistair Begg with Elizbeth McQuoid, *Ruth* (London: Inter-varsity Press, 2017), 75.
18. "Quotes on Missions," Ministry127, accessed March 16, 2021, https://ministry127.com/resources/illustration/quotes-on-missions.

19. Warren Wiersbe, *This is the Life! Enjoying the Blessings and Privileges of Faith in Christ.* (Grand Rapids: Baker Books, 2004), 22.

CHAPTER 7: CONSIDER IT DONE

1. Quoted in James L. Nicodem, *Walk: How to Apply the Bible* (Chicago: Moody Publishers, 2013), 105.
2. Quoted by John Maxwell in *Success: One Day at a Time* (Nashville: J. Countryman, 2000), 9.
3. Phyllis Moir, *I Was Winston Churchill's Private Secretary* (New York: Wilfred Funk, Inc., 1941), 164.
4. Eileen Crossman, *Mountain Rain: A New Biography of James O. Fraser* (Robesonia, PA: 1984), 13–14.
5. Luke Kerr-Dineen, "14 Inspiring Arnold Palmer Quotes," March 15, 2017, https://www.usatoday.com/story/sports/ftw/2017/03/15/14-inspiring-arnold-palmer-quotes-about-life-golf-and-business/99206580/.
6. Recounted in Rick Ezell, *Defining Moments: How God Shapes Our Character Through Crisis* (Downers Groe, IL: InterVarsity Press, 2001), 40.
7. Quoted in S.H. Spurgeon, W.E. Gladstone and H.S. Curr, "Spurgeon and Gladstone," *The Baptist Quarterly,* 11, no.1–2 (1942), 52.
8. David Atkinson, *The Message of Ruth* in The Bible Speaks Today Series, ed. J.A. Motyer (Downers Grove, IL: IVP Academic, 1974), 137.
9. Paul E. Miller, *A Loving Life: In a World of Broken Relationships* (Wheaton, IL: Crossway, 2014), 170–171.
10. Miller, *A Loving Life,* 173.
11. Samuel Cox, ed., *The Expositor: Volume 2,* (London: Hodder and Stroughton, 1875), 370–371.
12. C.S. Lewis, *The Four Loves* ((New York: Harcourt, Brace, Jovanovich, 1960), 169–170.
13. Story recounted in Cyril J. Barber, *Ruth: A Story of God's Grace: An Expositional Commentary.* (Eugene, OR: Wipf and Stock Publishers, 1989), 103.
14. Source unknown.
15. Quoted in William Vanderbloemen and Warren Bird, *Next: Pastoral Succession that Works* (Grand Rapids: Baker Books, 2014), 263.
16. Noel Piper, "Sarah Edwards: Jonathan's Home and Haven," in *A God Entranced Vision of All Things: The Legacy of Jonathan Edwards,* eds., John Piper and Justin Taylor (Wheaton, IL: Crossway Books, 2004), 62.

17. Piper, "Sarah Edwards: Jonathan's Home and Haven," 62.
18. A.E. Winship's study is recounted in Elisabeth D. Dodds, *Marriage to a Difficult Man: The Uncommon Union of Jonathan and Sarah Edwards* (Laurel, MS: Audubon Press and Christian Book Service, 2005), 31–32.
19. Dodds, *Marriage to a Difficult Man,* 32.
20. "Wren's Epitaph," The New York Times (The New York Times, January 31, 1982), https://www.nytimes.com/1982/01/31/travel/l-wren-s-epitaph-195156.html.
21. C.H. Spurgeon, "John Ploughman's Talk; or, Plain Advice for Plain People," accessed March 25, 2021, https://archive.spurgeon.org/misc/plowman.php.

CHAPTER 8: EVERYBODY LOVES A HAPPY ENDING

1. Finlo Rohrer, "Why the Obsession with Happy Endings?," *BBC News Magazine*, April 1, 2009, http://news.bbc.co.uk/2/hi/uk_news/magazine/7976192.stm.
2. Illustration is recounted in Charles R. Swindoll, *Job: A Man of Heroic Endurance* (Nashville, TN: Thomas Nelson Publishers, 2004), 308.
3. "The Old Farmer and the Prayer," September 6, 2017, https://www.rosebudnews.net/opinion/old-farmer-and-prayer.
4. David Strain, *Ruth and Esther: There is a Redeemer & Sudden Reversals* (Ross-shire, Scottland: Christian Focus Publications, 2018), 77.
5. *Little Women,* directed by Greta Gerwig (Sony Pictures, 2019).
6. United States Joint Economic Committee, "The Demise of the Happy Two-Parent Home," The Demise of the Happy Two-Parent Home - The Demise of the Happy Two-Parent Home - United States Joint Economic Committee, July 23, 2020, https://www.jec.senate.gov/public/index.cfm/republicans/2020/7/the-demise-of-the-happy-two-parent-home?fbclid=IwAR1jCsk4L__ydljFo3UKpGLJVeF1fCgpWefU6EPc27NUZAXMqnwxnl-hL4A.
7. David Atkinson, *The Message of Ruth.* (Downers Grove, IL: InterVarsity Press, 1983), 149.
8. Source unknown.
9. Schumacher's talk is recounted by Melvin Tinker in "Bridge Building and Preaching," accessed March 23, 2021, http://beginningwithmoses.org/oldsite/bigger/tinker_bridgebuilding.htm.

10. J. Carl Laney, "The Abortion Epidemic: America's Silent Holocaust," in *Bibliotheca Sacra,* 139 (1982), 348.
11. Ronald B. Allen, *In Celebrating Love of Life* (Portland, OR: Western Conservative Baptist Seminary, 1977), 6.
12. Mark Molloy, "Motorist Wakes up to Find Council Has Painted Disabled Bay around His Car… and given Him Fine," The Telegraph (Telegraph Media Group, April 5, 2016), https://www.telegraph.co.uk/news/2016/04/05/motorist-outraged-after-council-paints-disabled-bay-around-car-w/.
13. R. Albert Mohler, Jr., *The Gathering Storm: Secularism, Culture and the Church.* (Nashville, TN: Thomas Nelson Publishers, 2020), 40.
14. Erik Raymond, "What Does It Mean to Be the Apple of God's Eye?," The Gospel Coalition, August 16, 2017, https://www.thegospelcoalition.org/blogs/erik-raymond/what-does-it-mean-to-be-the-apple-of-gods-eye/.
15. Daniel L. Block, *Ruth: The King Is Coming* in Zondervan Exegetical Commentary on the Old Testament: A Discourse Analysis of the Hebrew Bible (Grand Rapids: Zondervan, 2015), 246.
16. Quoted in John Graham, *Thoughts for Each Step… Every Day* (Self-Published, 2015), 241.
17. James S. Hewett, *Illustrations Unlimited: A Topical Collection of Hundreds of Stories, Quotations and Humor* (Carol Stream, IL: Tyndale House Publishers, 1988), 197.

CONCLUSION

1. Paraphrased from Mark Steyn, Speech in Hollywood, 2016.